The Vietnam War: The Story and Photographs

Also by the Authors:

The Way It Was: Pearl Harbor, The Original Photographs (1991)
D-Day Normandy: The Story and Photographs (1993)
"Nuts!": The Battle of the Bulge (1994)
Rain of Ruin: The Hiroshima and Nagasaki Atomic Bombs (1995)

By Donald M. Goldstein and Katherine V. Dillon
The Williwaw War (1992)
The Pearl Harbor Papers: Inside the Japanese Plans (1993)
Amelia: A Centennial Biography (1997)

(With Gordon W. Prange)
At Dawn We Slept: The Untold Story of Pearl Harbor (1981)
Miracle at Midway (1982)
Target Tokyo: The Story of the Sorge Spy Ring (1984)
Pearl Harbor: The Verdict of History (1987)
December 7, 1941: The Day the Japanese Attacked Pearl Harbor (1988)
God's Samurai: Lead Pilot at Pearl Harbor (1990)

(With Masataka Chihaya)
Fading Victory: The Diary of Admiral Matome Ugaki (1991)

By J. Michael Wenger and Robert J. Cressman
Steady Nerves and Stout Hearts: The Enterprise (CV-6) *Air Group at Pearl Harbor,
7 December 1941* (1989)
Infamous Day: The Marines at Pearl Harbor, 7 December 1941 (1992)

By Donald M. Goldstein, Phil Williams, and J. M. Shafritz
Classic Readings of International Relations (1994)

By Donald M. Goldstein, Phil Williams, and Hank Andrews
Security in Korea: War, Stalemate and Negation (1994)

The Vietnam War: The Story and Photographs

by

DONALD M. GOLDSTEIN, KATHERINE V. DILLON,
and J. MICHAEL WENGER

BRASSEY'S

BRASSEY'S, INC.
P.O. Box 960
Herndon, VA 20172

Library of Congress Cataloging-in-Publication Data

Goldstein, Donald M.
            The Vietnam war : the story and photographs / by Donald M.
Goldstein, Katherine V. Dillon, and J. Michael Wenger.
                    p.   cm.
            Includes bibliographical references and index.
            1. Vietnamese Conflict, 1961–1975. 2. Vietnamese Conflict 1961–1975—Pictorial works.
I. Dillon, Katherine V. II. Wenger, J. Michael. III. Title.
DS557.7.G6   1997
959.704'3—dc21   97-11574
                                                                         CIP

ISBN 1-57488-210-4 (alk.paper)

Printed in the United States of America on acid-free paper that meets the American National Standards Institute Z39-48 Standard.

10 9 8 7 6 5 4 3 2 1

Preface

This book is the fifth in the Brassey's series of photographic books entitled, America Goes to War. The previous volumes were *The Way It Was: Pearl Harbor, The Original Photographs; D-Day Normandy: The Story and Photographs; "Nuts!": The Battle of the Bulge; and Rain of Ruin: The Hiroshima and Nagasaki Atomic Bombs.* Three others are planned: one on the Cold War, a 50th anniversary volume on the Korean War, and a special 100th anniversary volume on the Spanish-American War.

We have divided the current volume into eleven chapters. Chapter 1, "Background to Involvement," describes some of the background events that led to the French defeat and eventually to the American involvement. Chapter 2, "The Land and the People," gives a glimpse of how strange this land must have looked to the American soldiers newly arrived from home. Chapter 3, "The Antagonists," introduces some of the more prominent figures, political and military, on both sides of the conflict. Chapter 4, "America Commits to the Fight," covers events from the French withdrawal from Vietnam until the end of 1965, showing how the United States moved deeper and deeper into the conflict. Chapter 5, "Tools of War," briefly describes the major weapons and support equipment used by both armed forces. The increasing activity of 1966 and 1967 is covered in chapter 6, "Escalation." Chapter 7, "Life in a Strange Land," provides some insight into what life was like for a U.S. fighting man in Vietnam. Chapter 8, "Reconsideration and Vietnamization," deals with the climactic year 1968, and the subsequent gradual decrease in the war's momentum. This continues in chapter 9, "Wind Down and Withdrawal," which ends with the exchange of prisoners of war in 1973. In chapter 10, "The End," the Americans are out of Vietnam, and the communists promptly take over South Vietnam. Chapter 11, "Aftermath," pictures Ho Chi Minh City today, and the gradual reconciliation of the American people with their Vietnam veterans.

While we have attempted to present the story in the context of its political and diplomatic background, our focus is primarily on the American fighting men—the soldiers, airmen, sailors, and marines who bore the burden of battle, all too often in the face of indifference or downright hostility at home.

This is our first pictorial history that does not deal with World War II. The difference was immediately apparent and presented us with a problem in psychological orientation. World War II, however big the sacrifices involved, left the United States with the solid satisfaction of having helped rid the world of an unspeakable evil. In Vietnam, on the contrary, the final outcome was exactly what it would have been had the United States never sent South Vietnam a man, a dollar, or a piece of equipment—the communists took over.

In World War II, the fighting man was respected, even loved. The home folks showered him with letters and parcels, entertained him in their homes, volunteered with service organizations. In the Vietnam War, the "grunt" was barely tolerated, his morale was undermined by the press, Hollywood stars visiting Hanoi, college students demonstrating, and Washington waffling.

During World War II, the occupied nations were valiant partners, as eager to be free as the Allied armies were to free them. In South Vietnam, however, it often seems that few cared one way or the other. Top officials of the South Vietnamese government were more concerned with consolidating their positions—with their official and unofficial perquisites—than with providing responsible leadership. As for the South Vietnamese army's officers, one statistic tells it all—in 1966 Americans learned that "only one Vietnamese field grade officer [i.e., with a rank of major, lieutenant colonel, or colonel] had been wounded in action since 1954."[*]

The war in Vietnam violated more than one precept of conventional warfare. For instance, in conventional warfare, soldiers wear uniforms, and if caught out of uniform by the enemy can be shot as a spy. The Vietcong, however, dressed in the garb of the local peasants and after a raid blended into the landscape.

---

[*]Frances Fitzgerald. *Fire in the Lake: The Vietnamese and the Americans in Vietnam.* Boston: Little, Brown, 1972, p. 320.

More important, the theaters of operation in World War II had well-defined fronts—indicated by lines on maps—that defined the area of combat. A's forces were on one side; B's on the other. A's task was to force B back; B's to force A back. Both sides knew where they were. This was where the action was. This was the pattern of experience; officers were trained to expect it and deal with it. In Vietnam there was no front. Indeed, there had been no set-piece engagement since the French defeat at Dien Bien Phu in 1954.

All told, it was a whole new ball game, disconcerting for the American players and sometimes difficult for the historian trying in a modest way to make sense of the situation.

The story of the Vietnam War is not a pretty one, but it is by no means as ugly as certain Hollywood individuals, happily rewriting history to suit their purposes, would have us believe. We hope herein to give the reader a realistic look at the conflict as the fighting man saw it.

All times herein are local. This book is not footnoted, but we have included a brief bibliography for the convenience of those who wish to pursue this subject in greater depth.

All pictures are in the public domain and can be found in the National Archives, except 2-1, 2-15, and 2-20, courtesy of Col. James D. Blundell, USA (Ret.); 9-23, 9-43, and 9-44, courtesy of the Bruce Steele, *University Times*, University of Pittsburgh; 11-1 through 11-14 which were furnished by Dr. Max Brandt, University of Pittsburgh Semester at Sea Program; 11-15 through 11-17, in the Office Collection.

We would also like to acknowledge gratefully the invaluable cooperation of Col. John C. House, USA; Maj. William A. Labarbera, USAF; Capt. Mack Davis, USMC; Capt. James P. Nelson, USMC; Sgt. Baldie Bissette, USMC; Sgt. Roger H. Barrow, USA; Robert J. Cressman, Contemporary History Branch, Naval Historical Center; Charles Halberiein, Curator Branch, Naval Historical Center; Leah Campos, Robert Mullins, and Kendall Stanley.

We respectfully dedicate this book to those Americans who served in the Vietnam War, especially to those who died.

DONALD M. GOLDSTEIN, Ph.D.
Professor of Public and
    International Affairs
University of Pittsburgh
Pittsburgh, Pennsylvania

KATHERINE V. DILLON
CWO, USAF (Ret.)
Arlington, Virginia

J. MICHAEL WENGER, M.A.
Raleigh, North Carolina

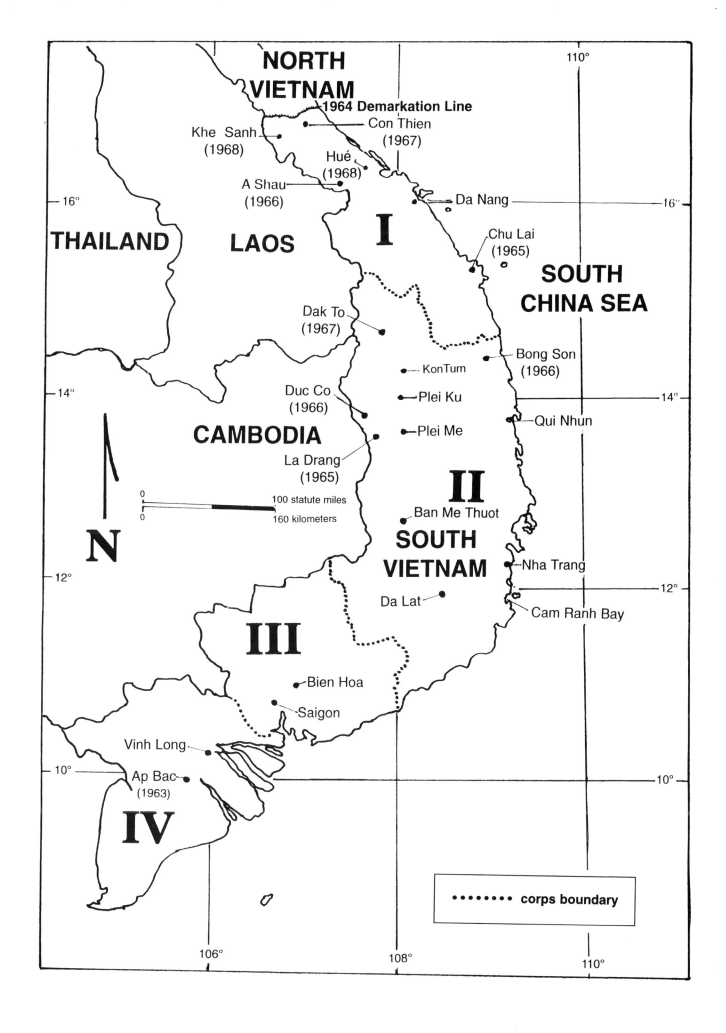

An AUSA Institute of Land Warfare Book

The Association of the United States Army, or AUSA, was founded in 1950 as a nonprofit organization dedicated to education concerning the role of the U.S. Army, to providing material for military professional development, and to the promotion of proper recognition and appreciation of the profession of arms. Its constituencies include those who serve in the Army today, including Army National Guard, Army Reserve, and Army civilians, the retirees and veterans who have served in the past, and all their families. A large number of public-minded citizens and business leaders are also an important constituency. The Association seeks to educate the public, elected and appointed officials, and leaders of the defense industry on crucial issues involving the adequacy of our national defense, particularly those issues affecting land warfare.

In 1988, AUSA established within its existing organization a new entity known as the Institute of Land Warfare. ILW's mission is to extend the educational work of AUSA by sponsoring a wide range of publications, to include books, monographs, and essays on key defense issues, as well as workshops, symposia, and since 1992, a television series. Among the volumes chosen as "An AUSA Institute of Land Warfare Book" are both new texts and reprints of titles of enduring value. Topics include history, policy issues, strategy, and tactics. Publication as an AUSA Book does not indicate that the Association of the United States Army and the publisher agree with everything in the book but does suggest that AUSA and the publisher believe the book will stimulate the thinking of AUSA members and others concerned about important defense-related issues.

Contents

Introduction

The Vietnam War was arguably the most traumatic experience for the United States in the twentieth century. That is indeed a grim distinction in a span that included two world wars, the assassinations of two presidents and the resignation of another, the Great Depression, the Cold War, racial unrest, and the drug and crime waves. In those disasters there was a shared national reaction. Especially in the two major wars, Americans in general believed their cause was just, their presence necessary to save humanity from a very real evil, hence worth the cost, however heartwrenching, of final victory. No such sense of mission animated the public over Vietnam, and the public's initial support of the government's policy eroded as the commitment in Vietnam gradually increased over the years with no end in sight.

The background of U.S. involvement in Vietnam extended many years into the past. For much of its history Vietnam was under Chinese control. In 1858 the French began their conquest of the area, and within thirty years had established protectorates in Tonkin and Annam in the northern sections, with Cochin-China in the south. The Japanese took over in World War II and set up a puppet regime under Bao Dai, former emperor of Annam. The Vietnamese forced him out in 1945.

Following World War II, from 1946 through 1954, the French made a determined effort to regain their former colonial possession. By late 1950, the French military was in a chaotic state. Troops were demoralized and their leaders were ineffective. The French called on their greatest soldier, General Jean de Lattre de Tassigny, to turn things around. He did his best—and de Lattre's best was very good indeed—but unfortunately for the French he died of cancer in January 1952, and his successors were not of his caliber. Final defeat came at Dien Bien Phu on May 8, 1954, at the hands of the communists under their brilliant general, Vo Nguyen Giap.

Under the cease-fire of July 21, 1954, French troops left the North, which a buffer zone separated from the South. Elections were to determine the form of government. The communists took over the country north of the 17th parallel and established a communist regime, with headquarters at Hanoi and, inevitably, headed by Ho Chi Minh. All Vietnamese in the North were not enchanted with the arrangement; approximately 900,000 fled south, most of them Roman Catholics. After several months under an interim government, led by Bao Dai, Premier Ngo Dinh Diem announced the formation of the Republic of Vietnam with himself as president.

North Vietnam lost no time setting out to conquer the South, at first through support of the southern communists, the Vietcong. This phase continued through the 1950s and early 1960s. In November 1963 Diem was overthrown and assassinated; the next year the North began a major drive into the South, strengthened by arms provided by the Chinese and Russians.

Throughout this period the United States regarded these developments with increasing alarm. Ho Chi Minh's forces were to be taken seriously. They had already defeated a major European power and obviously posed a sharp danger to South Vietnam. The United States gradually increased the level of its aid and support to South Vietnam, fearing the extension of communism into all of Indochina.

It is important to remember that those who formulated the "contain communism" policy and the "domino effect" theory were sincerely convinced—not without cause—that the free world was in danger. Communism was riding high in those days. After winning the respect of the world for its valiant struggle against Hitler's Nazis—a struggle that owed much to plain, old-fashioned patriotism—the Soviet Union had taken over or exported its creed to most of Eastern Europe. China, the most populous nation on earth, had gone communist; the Korean War and a communist Cuba added to U.S. fears. One can readily understand why those in charge of foreign affairs in Washington would view with active alarm the prospect of first Indochina, then other Asian countries, falling into the communist camp.

On the other hand, overactivity might bring about an even worse calamity. If the United States attacked North Vietnam all out, might not China and the Soviet

Union come to the aid of their client state, thus triggering World War III? The attempt to find a course of action that could navigate safely and successfully between the twin perils prevented the Americans from developing a firm, unambiguous policy.

In coming to the aid of South Vietnam, the Americans took on an enormous cultural problem. In World Wars I and II, the cultural patterns of the U.S. Allies were similar to those of the United States. South Vietnamese culture, on the other hand, was something new and unsettling. Any attempt to portray that region as a courageous little democracy trying to maintain its national identity and popular government was foredoomed. South Vietnam had never been a separate, independent nation, and its people had no sense of nationhood. Their loyalty extended to their families and their small native towns; beyond those boundaries was foreign territory. Steeped for centuries in the Confucian ideal of a benevolent imperial system where each man and woman had a clearly defined place, they found the idea of representative government alien and downright frightening. If the majority could change the ruler, the chosen of Heaven, what happened to stability? All would be chaos.

Not surprisingly, what by Western standards was corruption, but by Eastern standards normal procedure, flourished in the South Vietnamese government. Historically, easterners have had little compunction about using public funds for personal gain. Indeed, many regarded public office as a license to do whatever they could for the benefit of their families. During the Vietnam War, untold tons of food and supplies intended for the people and the armed forces disappeared from normal channels to enrich various officials and their next of kin.

Top officials all too often were filled with ambition and the pride of office, completely lacking a sense of responsibility for the general welfare. They were highly suspicious of anyone who might supplant them; hence, doing an honest job of work was often.the surest way to be discharged or shunted into a meaningless post.

The Army of the Republic of Vietnam (ARVN) reflected the image of the civil government. On many occasions, when properly led, the soldiers fought well. But too often the officers were just as rapacious, just as lacking in patriotism, and just as irresponsible toward their duties and their men as were the civilian office-holders. Also the families of the soldiers frequently accompanied them into combat areas, which posed serious problems. If in sufficient numbers, they blocked the roads, and if a conflict arose between a soldier's military duty and his family, it was no contest-the family won hands down, so desertions were rampant.

It took no Nostradamus to predict the ultimate result. Not even the United States could forever hold together such a disorganized, unmotivated mass in the face of an opponent that knew exactly what it wanted and was willing to pay any price.

It would take the genius of Shakespeare to do justice to the drama of American involvement in Vietnam, its gradual escalation conveying the sense of inevitable tragedy, then the equally doom-laden, slow disengagement. Surely, President Lyndon Baines Johnson would have attracted the attention of the Bard, with his gift for incisive yet compassionate portrayal of the ambitions, fears, and torments of the powerful. There is no doubt that Johnson wished the Vietnam War would go away. Every escalation increased the number of U.S. casualties. The war drained funds and attention from his Great Society, the president's name for his programs for social justice and economic prosperity; it eroded the reservoir of good will he had gained when the American people wanted to give him a sporting chance at the presidency; and the liberal press, traditionally prone to give Democratic presidents the benefit of the doubt, became restive.

Johnson was exceedingly sensitive about his public image, and not inclined to antagonize the media. For example, during the communist Tet Offensive of 1968, which was widely reported as an American defeat, communist losses far exceeded those of the Americans and the ARVN. Johnson knew the facts; he could have made a brief public statement carrying with it the prestige of the presidency and straightened out the misunderstanding. Johnson ducked his duty and left the denials to the military, which did not carry the same clout, and indeed merely aroused suspicion.

Johnson had the means and the power to take the United States out of Vietnam, but he could not bring himself to become the first American president to lose a war. Instead, he pulled himself out of the running for a second full term and left the problem to Richard M. Nixon, who drew more flack winding down the commitment than Johnson had building it up.

During the last years of the war, a distressing situation arose. For the first time, the American people were not solidly behind their combat troops. Too many stories filtered out of sagging morale, lack of discipline, and even sabotage.

In 1969 Congress investigated the My Lai incident, which had taken place following the Tet Offensive. A company from the Americal Division, with no provocation, had massacred about three hundred civilians, mostly women and children, in the town of My Lai. Later attempts to justify the action as necessary for the safety of the soldiers cut no ice. The American people could not see how grandmothers and babies could menace American troops. One of the most horrifying aspects of this shocking incident was the reaction of the officer in charge, Lt. William Calley: "It was no big deal."

My Lai was so out of character that the congressional investigating committee suggested that there was "a question as to the legal sanity at the time of those men involved." Psychologists did not agree. But with all due respect to their expertise, it would be easy to conclude that a kind of mass mental detachment afflicted many of the American troops. They had been posted to a country as alien as Mars, with no front and rear areas, where friend and enemy looked exactly alike and might be interchangeable, where every stretch of jungle or head-high elephant grass could conceal a single sniper or a sizable Vietcong or North Vietnamese Army (NVA) unit—these and other factors could readily lead to paranoia. Drugs were available and thousands succumbed to their lure. In the latter years of the war, there also was a significant increase in what the men called fragging; that is, the killing of officers and noncommissioned officers (NCOs) by their own men. Isolated examples of this type of murder have taken place in all wars, but the fact that in Vietnam it occurred frequently enough to gain a nickname revealed how far private morality and military discipline had eroded.

Also for the first time, a draft dodger was not always a figure of contempt. Those who avoided military service, while disapproved of by the majority, who still believed the country deserved support, had a substantial backing among those determined to force a U.S. withdrawal from Vietnam, no matter how.

Part of the mechanics of pullout was the program known as Vietnamization. Ostensibly the idea was to prepare the people, government, and armed forces of South Vietnam to carry on alone. The actual objective was to disentangle the United States. Even had it been an honest effort by the United States to train the South Vietnamese, it was hopeless. It was not the fault of the South Vietnamese people, who were intelligent and industrious. Rather it was because Vietnamization was more than just instruction in techniques and methodology; it called for a complete turnaround of the national orientation. On the practical level, South Vietnam lacked the industrial base to manufacture and maintain the weapons of modern warfare as well as provide a level of livelihood so necessary for a thriving society. The main ingredient of Vietnamization was time. Given years, perhaps decades, it might have been successful. But time was precisely what was lacking.

By the time that Vietnamization was promulgated, it had dawned on the battered North Vietnamese, with what incredulous relief and exultation one can only imagine, that military engagements, whether victories or defeats, were irrelevant. As with the French, the real battle was being fought on their enemy's home front—in Congress, in the press, on television, on campuses, and in public meetings—and North Vietnam was winning. A military victory or two might give Hanoi a few bargaining chips at the cease-fire negotiations, but this was not really necessary. The United States had lost whatever will to win it had ever possessed, and wanted only to get out.

After lengthy and maddening negotiations, a cease-fire was signed on January 27, 1973, to which North Vietnam subsequently paid no attention. Following a building-up period, North Vietnamese forces attacked the South early in 1975, and South Vietnam surrendered on April 30 of that year. On July 2, 1976, North and South were officially united as a communist state.

Unsung in this bitter defeat, and only now in the 1990s receiving public recognition and gratitude for their sacrifices, are the millions of Americans who served in and around Vietnam from 1960 to 1975. They did their duty and honored their country's commitment, sometimes at the cost of their lives, in an unpopular cause. The Vietnam War Memorial in Washington D.C., honors the war's dead with a cool, dignified, black marble wall etched with their names. This volume seeks to remember those Americans lost and also to remember all those who served well and faithfully, and returned home.

Chapter 1
Background to Involvement

With World War II over, the French hoped and expected to return to their former colonies in French Indochina, pick up the pieces, and carry on as before. This attitude was uncharacteristically naive of the French, who prided themselves on their reason and logic. Both of these virtues should have convinced them that the broken threads of history are not so easily rewoven. But France's national pride, so sorely humiliated in World War II, surely played a role.

The natives of Indochina had no reason to love and welcome back their former European masters. And if they had cherished any hope during World War II that the Greater East Asia Co-Prosperity Sphere would be an improvement, the Japanese soon disillusioned them. Their fellow Asians proved just as rapacious, just as indifferent to the natives' needs, and considerably more cruel than the French. It is no wonder the natives were in a mood to echo Mercutio's curse: "A plague on both your houses!"

Anticipating the return of the French, the Vietnamese, Khmer (Cambodians), and Pathet Lao (Laotians) put aside their disagreements to form a unit-ed front in their struggle for independence. It is significant that in May 1951 they held a conference the in People's Republic of China (1-1). Active resistance would be largely communist.

This conference came fairly late in the first Vietnamese War—that between the French and the Vietminh. Diplomacy had failed; the Vietnamese would settle for nothing less than full independence, which the French refused to grant. Fighting began in late autumn of 1946. In early 1947 the French seemed well on the way to victory. Ho Chi Minh's headquarters had been driven out of Hanoi and major cities cleared of Vietminh. But the French failed to make the early drive that could have secured final victory. The monsoon season was just two months away, and instead of launching a quick push, the French decided to wait until the end of the monsoons, in the autumn; this cost them valuable time and enabled the communists to build up a much more formidable force.

We cannot go here into the details of the first Vietnam War, which dragged on for six years. With slow inevitability the French weakened and the Vietminh grew

1-1 The People's Republic of China, May 1951. Vietnamese, Cambodian, and Laotian representatives meet in China to plan a united front against the French. Here, senior delegates from Vietnam and Cambodia exchange gifts.

1-2 The French aircraft carrier _Arromanches_ steams in the Gulf of Tonkin during the struggle to maintain control over Indochina.

1-3 French coastal patrol vessels ply a river in Vietnam.

more skillful and confident. In one area the French had the edge. Their military, particularly the navy, could bring to bear sophisticated hardware, much of which was American-made, including F-6F Hellcat fighters, Curtiss SB2C Helldiver dive bombers, Sikorsky helicopters, and escort ships (1-2).

Command of the sea off Vietnam, however, did not mean to Vietnam what command of the sea would have meant to an island nation, for instance, Great Britain. True, the French could bring in weapons, but they could not blockade the Vietminh, who were supplied by land from China. One key French advantage amid a sea of disadvantages and shortcomings was partial control over Vietnam's inland waterways (1-3).

Land warfare became increasingly frustrating for the French beginning on July 28, 1953. Operation Camarque was designed to destroy the Vietminh 95th Regiment, which controlled Highway 1 and the area between Quang Tri City and Hué (1-4). There, the French encountered classic guerrilla fighting, facing hostile locals and an enemy that seemed to melt into the countryside. The French inflicted some damage, but not enough to destroy the 95th, and after several days broke off the engagement. The French fighting men called the nearby segment of highway "The Street Without Joy."

The war in Vietnam posed a foreign relations problem for the United States. On the one hand, Franco-American friendship dated back to the American Revolution; French and Americans had been comrades-in-arms in two world wars; Americans had suffered in spirit with the French during the Nazi occupation. Did not these ties impose a certain obligation? Moreover, the French in Indochina were fighting communists, and hence, automatically, were allies in policy.

On the other hand, the position of France as an anti-communist champion was shaky. The Communist Party was strong in France; communists had been a powerful force in the Resistance; and France had come close to

1–4 French and Vietnamese forces advance inland during Operation Camarque on Vietnam's central coast on August 25, 1953.

going communist after the war. From that angle, the French in Vietnam were not so much attempting to contain communism as to regain their Asian colonies; although their army was incapable of doing this. Moreover, neocolonialism was repugnant to many Americans. Why should the United States—of all nations—assist the French in this unwise attempt to turn back the clock? Also, the natives' standard of living in Indochina had not improved under French rule.

The United States tried to strike a balance by supplying the French with arms while avoiding direct involvement. By March 1954, Giap's forces were besieging Dien Bien Phu in what promised to be a military classic-a decisive battle. On March 20, General Paul Ely, chief of staff of the French armed forces, went to Washington to seek increased U.S. assistance (1-5). He wanted more aircraft—which he got—and a commitment that the United States would intervene if China entered the war—which he did not. This was a remote contingency at the time. Why should the canny Chinese go to war on behalf of their clients, who already had the French on the ropes?

Admiral Arthur W. Radford, chairman of the Joint Chiefs of Staff, suggested a series of raids by B-29s from the Philippines against the besiegers. But this action might draw the Chinese into the war, and no one could guarantee success. If the raids failed, what then? Ground forces? None of the other service chiefs supported the suggestion, and after considerable high-level discussion President Dwight D. "Ike" Eisenhower rejected the proposition. In any case, the operation would have been too late to save Dien Bien Phu, which was taken on May 8, 1954.

1-5 Washington, late March 1954. General Paul Ely (center), French Armed Forces Chief of Staff, shares a cordial moment with President Eisenhower (left) and Admiral Arthur W. Radford (right), chairman of the U.S. Joint Chiefs of Staff. (See also photograph 1-8)

A cease-fire was signed in Geneva, Switzerland, on July 21, 1954. The communists gained control north of the 17th parallel, and elections were to be held to determine what type of government the rest of the country preferred. As mentioned previously, this cease-fire was followed by a massive southward exodus of refugees (1-6). It is unlikely that Ho Chi Minh regretted their loss; communism had no use for dissidents, and these emigrants were passionate in their anticommunism (1-7 and 1-8).

The agreement reached in Geneva was a notable victory for Ho Chi Minh (1-9). He, Giap and his other

1-6 Refugee fishermen flee to the South from communist-controlled North Vietnam.

1-7 Immigrants from the North served to strengthen the already conservative populace of the South.

leaders had built from scratch an army that had humbled a great Western power (1-10) and secured Vietnamese independence.

The United States could—and should—have learned much from the French debacle. All the ingredients for defeat were there—the country not wholeheartedly behind the effort, the government indecisive and failing to give the military clear-cut objectives, unrealistic strategy, and a disastrous underestimation of their opponent.

In the South, Emperor Bao Dai became head of state with Ngo Dinh Diem as prime minister. During 1955 Diem crossed swords with the Binh Xuyen, an influential gang of bandits that controlled much of Saigon and

was financed by enormous sums from the gambling and protection rackets. Bao Dai, who had been supporting the Binh Xuyen, ordered Diem to return to France. Diem refused; his break with Bao Dai plus the success of the regular army in driving the Binh Xuyen out of Saigon opened the path for Diem's eventual assumption of power (1-11).

General J. Lawton Collins, who was in Saigon as Eisenhower's representative, did not have faith in Diem's ability and suggested to Washington that the government support someone else (1-12). The Binh Xuyen incident intervened, however, and the Americans decided to continue to support Diem. On October 16, 1955, Diem pro-

1-8 U.S. ambassador Donald Heath joins Saigon mayor Ngo Dinh Diem in 1954 in welcoming the 100,000th northern refugee to freedom in the South.

1-10 Stern-faced victors and vanquished. Following the French collapse at Dien Bien Phu in 1954, a French commander turns over his garrison to a representative of the Democratic Republic of Vietnam.

1-9 Vietnam, May 1954. President Ho Chi Minh with two children who presented him with flowers. "Uncle Ho" loved to be photographed with children, although in conducting national affairs he easily shed this avuncular veneer.

claimed the establishment of the Republic of Vietnam and became its president.

Ho Chi Minh had no intention of coexisting with a Vietnamese republic in the South and made his preparations patiently, solidifying his relationships with other communist regimes (1-13 and 1-14). Fighting between North and South had persisted since 1954. On December 31, 1959, the North adopted a communist constitution calling for reunification of the country under the leadership of the North. This caused great concern in the United States and eventually led to the Americans joining the war directly.

1-11 President Diem enjoys a cruise on a river patrol vessel following the defeat of the Binh Xuyen sect in 1955. Although Vietnamese man the vessel, American and British military observers are present in the stern.

1-12 President Diem and General J. Lawton Collins discuss the Saigon situation at Independence Palace on May 13, 1955.

1-14 Ho Chi Minh curries favor with President Sukarno of Indonesia during a state visit on March 10, 1959.

1-13 Ho Chi Minh arrives in Warsaw, Poland, for an official state visit. Beside him to his right is Polish Chief of State Alexander Zawadski.

Chapter 2
The Land and the People

Vietnam encompasses about 127,000 square miles of territory, about the size of New Mexico, but very different in shape. It forms a long, narrow strip on the east coast of the Indochinese Peninsula, its coast about 1,400 miles long. To the north is China, to the west are Laos and Cambodia. Physically it is a country with mountains, tropical rain forest, and arable land. Rice is its major crop.

Vietnam was primarily a country of peasants, whose lives followed a local, seasonal orbit (2-1). They had no sense of nationhood and their patriotism constituted loyalty to their families, their plots of land, and their villages. A small farmer in the United States, or any other Western nation, could and frequently did take a keen, intelligent interest in who was running the government and how. Feeling himself part of a nation with a way of life and a political system both familiar and cherished, he would resist any attempt to overthrow them with every means at his disposal.

The individual Vietnamese peasant, however, was likely to give his loyalty to whomever treated him well, and frequently that was the Vietcong guerrillas. Although village leaders such as chiefs, teachers and priests were often targets of communist assassination, the Vietcong leaders wisely instructed their troops to treat the general peasantry kindly. On the other hand, ARVN troops, conscious of belonging to the government, all too often behaved arrogantly and contemptuously toward the villagers. The villagers made their choice on the basis of personal experience.

Photograph 2-2 records a seemingly pleasant encounter—but who knew what the morrow would bring? Many veterans still harbor a deep paranoia, born in no small measure of their ambivalent relationship with the Vietnamese civilian population.

Between 85 and 90 percent of the population was Vietnamese, with a sprinkling of other ethnic groups. These in turn were subdivided, as for example the

2-1 A woman crushes rice as Vietnamese peasants have for centuries.

2-2 A member of the 9th Infantry Division and a Vietnamese scout talk with a peasant family during a mission south of Thoi Tan Island.

2-3 A Montagnard elder says a prayer before a sacrificial altar during a ceremony where the various Montagnard villages pledge loyalty to the Vietnamese central government.

Montagnards, who spoke several different dialects. These "mountain people" (2-3) proved loyal to the South Vietnamese government, and had a particularly close relationship to U.S. Special Forces operating in the Central Highlands.

One of the more numerous minorities was the Chinese, who had exercised an influence far out of proportion to their numbers. For years the Chinese had controlled most of Vietnam's trade and commerce. A new group of Chinese crossed the border into Vietnam after the communists took over China; then, after the Vietminh conquered the French, they moved once more, this time into South Vietnam. These immigrants called themselves the "Hai Yen," and were a source of anti-communist support in the South.

In addition to ethnic diversity, Vietnam had a mixture of religions. Buddhists and Taoists were by far the most numerous, but there was also a strong Catholic

2-4 Church services in the village of Binh Hung, a locality with a large Chinese population.

influence (2-4 and 2-5). Catholicism did not arrive with the French, it preceded them. It had been reports from missionaries working in the region that attracted French attention to an area of potential colonialism. Among the approximately one million who fled North Vietnam following the French defeat were many Catholics who were unwilling to take their chances with the communists.

Of all the victims of this long-drawn-out, cruel war, none were more pathetic than the children, innocent and uncomprehending victims of their elders' greed and savagery. The suffering of such little ones, as appear in 2-6 made a deep and lasting impression on American servicemen.

In North Vietnam, everything and everyone had its place in the communist scheme of things, including the young people, who performed their civil duty by parading in the streets of Hanoi (2-7).

A major feature of Vietnam's geography is the delta of the Mekong River, which empties into the South China Sea southwest of Saigon (2-8). The river and the monsoon rains ensure that this area is constantly damp and occasionally in flood (2-9 and 2-10).

Vegetation grows lushly throughout much of Vietnam, and posed a real problem for military movements. The ubiquitous elephant grass seemed to grow any place not under cultivation (2-11). Not only was it difficult to get through, it was high enough to conceal an entire military unit within yards of its opponents. Equally troublesome were the rice paddies (2-12), whose crazy quilt pattern of inundated fields not only hindered movement but also was very susceptible to booby traps along the narrow paths. These booby traps, which never

2-5 A young girl from a mission school in Bien Hoa province sits in the lap of Charles M. Muscat.

2-6 Vietnamese orphans, whose parents were killed by Vietcong forces—one who lost a limb in an ambush, and two polio victims.

2-7 During the mid-1960s, uniformed students parade in Hanoi carrying a portrait of Ho Chi Minh.

2-8 A portion of the Mekong Delta between My Tho and Vinh Long.

2-9 The monsoon rains flood the streets of Chau Doc City in the Mekong Delta, 120 miles southwest of Saigon.

2-10 Civilians in Long An province assist regional forces in crossing one of that area's countless streams.

seemed to "get the locals," were yet another factor that fed paranoia and distrust on the part of the Americans.

Not much more hospitable than the wet, overgrown lowlands were the rugged mountains, where roads were almost nonexistent. These nearly impassable ranges ran the length of the country (2-13) and in places seemed to rise out of the sea (2-14). The famous Ho Chi Minh Trail, the route North Vietnam used to supply communist forces in the South, ran roughly near the western edge of these mountains, mostly in Laos.

To the American soldier, the typical Vietnamese architecture must have seemed like that of another world, or at least a step backward in time, not by years, but by centuries. Rural buildings were usually constructed of mud and bamboo, with a roof thatched with palm branches (2-15). In the cities, on the other hand, years of French occupation had left their mark; there were fine homes and other buildings constructed in the French style (2-16).

Indeed, Vietnam's cities offered many examples of the mixture of old and new. In photograph 2-17, a taxi speeds past a venerable Buddhist temple. The glamour of an earlier day and another life style typified Hué, the old imperial capital. Like many capital cities that have outlived their political significance, Hué had a special nostalgic charm that was missing in Saigon and Hanoi. But even Hué was not immune to the changing times, as evidenced by the modern building on the waterfront in the lower right of photograph 2-18.

Under the French, Saigon, the bustling capital of the South, had been called the "Paris of the Orient" (2-19). Unfortunately, as with all imitations, it lacked the essential character of the original. The French could construct boulevards (2-20) and impressive edifices such

2-11 SP4 William Langley of the 11th Armored Cavalry peers through the elephant grass near Fire Support Base Henderson.

2-12 Movement across country proved difficult in the rice paddies.

2-13 The mountainous terrain near Fire Support Base Action, seen on October 20, 1969.

2-14 Mountains seen from a guard tower at Fire Support Base Debbie near Duc Pho.

2-15 A small village outside Tra -On in the Mekong Delta.

2-16 A French-style house in the city of Can Tho in the heart of the Mekong Delta.

2-17 A Buddhist temple in Can Tho.

2-18 Hué, the old imperial Vietnamese capital, was a typically curious mixture of the very old and very new.

2-19 Saigon, seen here on December 7, 1966.

as the presidential palace (2-21) and the National Assembly Building (2-22), but they could not build a spirit. Paris had its share of high-crime areas and corruption, but the city was sound enough to survive them. In Saigon, under both the French and American occupations, corruption was a way of life, to the point where the city and the government could not function as the capital of a viable political entity.

A traffic jam on the "Street of Flowers" may well symbolize the congested, bustling state of South Vietnam's capital (2-23), while a contrasting scene in Hanoi (2-24), with its conspicuous lack of motor transport, paints a picture of austerity. Probably the citizens of Hanoi would have enjoyed some of the fleshpots of Saigon, but everything available went to support the war effort—which is one reason why Saigon today is called Ho Chi Minh City.

**2-20 The view up Le Loi Avenue
in Saigon, The Hotel Caravelle
is the tall building to the right.**

**2-21 Formerly the Opera House
during French rule, this building
became the Chamber of Deputies
after independence and then a
cultural center under the communists.**

2-22 Independence Palace.

2-23 Interminable traffic jams made a lasting impression on Americans stationed in Saigon.

2-24 "Rush hour" in Hanoi in 1965.

Chapter 3
The Antagonists

As with all wars, the Vietnam conflict brought into the public consciousness individuals who under normal circumstances would have been of little or no interest to the man in the street. For instance, Ho Chi Minh (3-1) no doubt would have been a significant figure in modern Asian history had he chosen, let us say, a Gandhi-like path of passive resistance, but his name would not have become the household word it was in the United States for a good two decades.

Ho Chi Minh was born in 1890 in Nghe An province, and given the name Nguyen Sinh Cung. His father was the son of a concubine and thus low on the social scale. He must have been a man of considerable ability, however, because by assiduous study, he eventually became a mandarin in the court at Hué. He left this position suddenly, abandoning his wife and three children for the life of an itinerant teacher/healer. His father's actions may provide insight into why Ho had so little of the family feeling that is so strong among Vietnamese. He never married and seemingly had little to do with any of his relatives.

At the age of twenty-one Ho signed on board a French freighter and for the next thirty years wandered about France, England, the United States, the Soviet Union, China, and Siam, under such an assortment of names that it is a wonder his biographers were later able to follow his movements. During those years he learned to speak fluent French, English, Russian, Siamese, and several Chinese dialects.

Ironically, the longer he stayed away from his homeland the more patriotic he became. He embraced communism because it seemed to him to offer the best means toward an independent Vietnam. Early in 1941 he crossed the Chinese border into Vietnam where he met with several colleagues and founded the Vietnamese Independence League, popularly known as the Vietminh. He then adopted his last pseudonym, Ho Chi Minh, which means something like Light-Bringer.

There is no question that Ho was a gifted leader. He was not physically prepossessing—a very thin little man suffering from tuberculosis—but he had that elusive charismatic quality that draws men. He also could

3-1 Ho Chi Minh, president of communist North Vietnam, shown here in July 1957.

be ruthless. In 1925 he betrayed a colleague to the authorities in Shanghai for 100,000 piastérs, later claiming that the man's arrest would stir up much-needed resentment in Vietnam, and Ho needed the money for his communist organization.

With a combination of natural acumen, an excellent intelligence network, leadership, and circumstances, Ho reached the point where on September 2, 1945, he declared Vietnam independent. His declaration's opening sentence quoted the American Declaration of Independence. Ho did not live to see the full fruition of his mission, however; he died on September 2, 1969—the 24th anniversary of his declaration.

Maj. Gen. Tran Van Tra (3-2) was a relative new-comer to the scene, and he was by birth a southerner, having been born in Quang-ngai province in central Vietnam. He joined the Vietminh, which, following the partition of Vietnam in 1954, sent him first to North Vietnam, then to China and the Soviet Union for train-ing. He must have done well, because within nine years he was at the head of the Vietcong in the Mekong Delta. Another nine years and he had risen to command the B-2 front, comprising South Vietnam below the Central Highlands.

Tra did not remain in favor after final victory, how-ever. He had led the attack against Saigon during the 1968 Tet Offensive, and in 1982 he published a book that harshly criticized the Tet Offensive as ill-conceived, hav-ing been founded "in part on our illusions based on our subjective desires." As a result, he claimed, the campaign had set objectives beyond the NVA's capability, while far underestimating those of the enemy, leading to heavy NVA and Vietcong losses.

General Tra may have believed himself safe, even praiseworthy, in thus pointing out errors from which lessons could be learned. Such searching criticism of one's self and one's comrades was an important indoctri-nation tool at the lower levels of the armed forces, but Tra swiftly learned that what was sauce for the troops was not necessarily sauce for the brass. Tra's criticism of Tet and other exposures of the Hanoi establishment as less than divinely inspired infuriated officials at all levels of the government, who tried—without success—to pre-vent copies of Tra's book from leaving Vietnam (it would become a valuable source book for future historians.) Tra vanished in 1982 or 1983.

Brig. Gen. Tran Do (3-3) was the third ranking offi-cer of the so-called Liberation Army of South Vietnam. He was considered one of North Vietnam's best soldiers, although he had questioned Hanoi's strategy, agreeing with Giap as early as 1946 on the importance of guerril-la warfare. Stanley Karnow described him as "a myste-rious figure cloaked in pseudonyms who was reported to have been killed several times."

General Vo Nguyen Giap (3-4) in many ways was the most interesting character of the Vietnam War. Conceded to be one of the twentieth century's top gen-erals, he never received formal instruction in military sci-ence. But he was by no means ignorant of the art of war, having studied on his own such authorities as Clausewitz and Sun Tzu as well as the statutory communist theo-rists. He admired Napoleon and T.E. Lawrence, and particularly the Vietnamese heroes of the past. In one

3-2 Maj. Gen. Tran Van Tra, Deputy Commander-in-Chief of the communist Liberation Army of South Vietnam. He was also a Central Committee member of the Lao Dong Party.

3-3 Brig. Gen. Tran Do, Deputy Commander-in-Chief of the Liberation Army of South Vietnam.

of his few genial moments, he described himself as "a self-taught general."

He was born in 1911 in the village of An Xa, just north of what would become the partition line between North and South Vietnam. He attended Quoc Hoc Academy in Hué, where he joined a group of nationalist youngsters and was expelled following a student strike. "Nationalism made me a Marxist," he later claimed. He earned a law degree at the University of Hanoi, a French institution, but never practiced. He also taught in a private school for a time.

Giap's first command was a band of thirty-four guerrillas, which he led to two small victories on Christmas Eve 1944. At the end of his career he commanded the world's third largest army, and Pham Van Dong, premier of North Vietnam, could justly hail him as "the architect of our victory."

3-4 General Vo Nguyen Giap (right), North Vietnamese vice-premier and minister of National Defense, chats with members of the People's Army in December 1965. Lt. Gen. Van Tien Dung, chief of the General Staff of the People's Army, trails behind.

He did not look the part, standing slightly under five feet tall—short even by Vietnamese standards—but seems to have enjoyed throwing his weight around. He could be arrogant, ruthless, and suspicious. He was also brilliant and totally dedicated to the cause of his fatherland.

At times Giap disagreed with official Hanoi policies. While all agreed on the objective—the conquest and unification of all Vietnam under a communist government—opinions differed as to the method. Giap was a "northerner"; that is, he believed that North Vietnam's first priority was to strengthen itself. The "southerners" wanted active warfare against South Vietnam. Although the southerners usually won the argument, Giap always commanded to the best of his ability, even when he disagreed with the decision.

Giap did have limitations. His lack of imagination kept him from understanding the potential of methods of warfare with which he had no direct experience, such as air and naval power. At times he made mistakes. But he defeated the French and the South Vietnamese, and although he did not take part in the final struggle, he was largely instrumental in defeating the Americans. He fell out of favor after the failure of the 1972 Easter Offensive, which he had advised against. However, he did not "disappear," and from all accounts enjoyed a comfortable retirement.

Shown in photograph 3-4 with Giap is his protégé, Lt. Gen. Van Tien Dung, the only member of Hanoi's politburo to come from a real peasant background. He had been chief of staff of the Vietminh army, in charge of logistics at the decisive battle of Dien Bien Phu. He replaced Giap in command of the NVA while the latter remained minister of defense. Dung became a full member of the politburo in August 1972, and he was an ideal partner for Giap. He was steady, and practical, and unlike Giap, he had considerable personal charm and wit.

From 1954 to 1963, the dominant figure in South Vietnam was Ngo Dinh Diem (3-5). He came from central Vietnam, the third of six sons born to a mandarin-class family that had been Catholic since the seventeenth century. He studied law and administration and at the age of twenty-five was a provincial governor; however, he quarreled with the French and passed about a decade in obscurity. At one point he was a prisoner of the Vietminh, but Ho Chi Minh ordered his release. Despite Ho's action, the Vietminh wanted him dead, and in 1950 Diem left Vietnam, spending two years at Maryknoll Seminary in New Jersey. There he met a number of prominent U.S. Catholics, such as then Senator John F.

3-5 President Ngo Dinh Diem visits with American Maj. Gen. Matthew H. Deichelmann during Air Force Day ceremonies in Saigon in June 1958.

Kennedy and Francis Cardinal Spellman, who became one of Diem's supporters.

In May 1953, Diem left for Europe, where Bao Dai, former Emperor of Annam, was living in France. Bao Dai had been Japan's puppet during the Japanese occupation of Vietnam. He abdicated in 1945, but the French brought him back, hoping he could focus anticommunist forces and, of course, do what the French told him to do. He lacked the character to be a leader, however, and much preferred to spend his time enjoying himself in France. From all accounts, his government in Vietnam was as corrupt as it was inept. Bao Dai and Diem each could use the other: Diem needed an official appointment as a springboard, and Bao Dai believed Diem could eventually gather strong American support. On June 18, 1954, the emperor appointed Diem prime minister. A little over a year later, Diem deposed Bao Dai and became president.

Publicly the United States supported Diem and lavished praise on him. President Lyndon Johnson, called him "the Churchill of the decade." Behind the scenes, it was a case of making do until someone better came along. On the surface Diem seemed promising; he was well-educated, a true nationalist equally opposed to the French and the communists, and his personal morals were in pleasing contrast to those of the playboy Bao Dai.

Disillusionment soon set in. Like Ho Chi Minh, Diem never married, but unlike Ho he did not hesitate to enrich his family at the expense of the nation. He became suspicious and devious, with his political survival at the top of his priorities. This fact undermined his ability as a wartime president because he wanted to avoid the criticism that would follow heavy casualties. His generals soon realized that caution rather than initiative was the watchword. By 1963 the Americans were seeking a replacement, and hinted to a junta of dissatisfied officers that the United States would not oppose a coup. On November 1, 1963, the officers ousted Diem, and the next day he and his unpopular brother, Ngo Dinh Nhu, were murdered.

Diem's immediate successors were no improvement. In 1965 General Nguyen Van Thieu (3-6) was elected president and remained in office for a decade. The youngest of five children, Thieu received his early education in a missionary school at Hué. For a short time he was with the Vietminh, then joined the French. He earned a commission in the French colonial army and was a good officer. He married into a Vietnamese Catholic family and converted to that faith. After the defeat of the French, the United States Military Assistance Advisory Group (MAAG) apparently tagged Thieu as promising, because they sent him to the United States for training.

Thieu recognized that he needed the Americans, but he did not trust them. He was by nature suspicious, a plotter rather than a leader. In 1967 Thieu, heretofore regarded as a figurehead chief of state with his premier, Air Vice Marshal Nguyen Cao Ky (3-7) as the real power, surprised everyone, including the Americans, by challenging Ky for the presidency. After much argument, anger, and tears on all sides, Ky agreed to take the vice presidency with a few other perquisites thrown in. Thieu won election by a surprisingly slim margin over a civilian candidate. Thieu held the office until April 12, 1975; the Vietnam War ended the following day.

Ky was a northerner by birth and the French trained him as a pilot. It was claimed that if it had wings and motive power, Ky could fly it. Only thirty-four years old when he became premier, Ky was a consciously picturesque figure in the tradition of pilots of the 1920s and early 1930s. He affected black or purple flying suits and pearl-handled revolvers. Although his experience did not seem to qualify him as a premier of a modern state, his government was surprisingly stable. He paid lip service to reform, founding the Anti-Fraud and Corruption League, but Thieu, with cause, disbanded it for fraud and corruption. Ky had no power to reform even had he so desired. Like all junta leaders he was captive to his subordinate commanders. At first he sought American approval, but then became resentful of U.S. dominance.

The war years saw a steady stream of leaders, civilian and military, on the American side. Unlike during other wars, no single political party controlled the government. Both Republicans and Democrats had their turns at the helm. On April 4, 1959, President Dwight D. Eisenhower (3-8) made the first commitment to maintain South Vietnam as a separate, noncommunist state. It was a small beginning; at the end of 1960, Eisenhower's last full year in office, there were only about 900 U.S. military personnel in Vietnam.

John F. Kennedy (3-9) inherited an unpleasant dilemma in regard to South Vietnam. If he did nothing and left that country to its fate, he would be remembered as the president—the Democratic president—who lost Southeast Asia, giving aid and comfort to the communists. If he went to the other extreme and committed a sizable number of U.S. combat troops and took effective

3-6 Nguyen Van Thieu, president of South Vietnam, answers questions at a press conference in June 1969.

action, he risked World War III, or at least the long-dreaded ground war on the Asian mainland. He compromised by sending two helicopter companies and increasing the scope of the MAAG. At that time, there was little idea of the American troops themselves engaging in combat. Kennedy was assassinated on November 22, 1963—just twenty days after Diem. At the end of that year, the U.S. military presence in Vietnam had reached 16,300.

Thrust into the presidency under distressing conditions, Lyndon Johnson (3-10) was not in an enviable position. He had to take over for an unusually popular president who had been diametrically different from him in style and personality. Of all the Kennedy inheritance, nothing gave Johnson more trouble than the Vietnam War. The ambiguous, don't-lose-but-don't-win-big policy was still in effect, his own interests were centered on domestic problems, and the antiwar faction was growing. Eventually Johnson bowed out rather than seek a second full term. Ironically, he was succeeded not by one of the committed antiwar candidates but by the anticommunist Richard M. Nixon.

3-7 Nguyen Cao Ky, premier of South Vietnam.

3-8 Dwight D. Eisenhower, president of the United States.

3-9 John F. Kennedy, president of the United States.

At the end of 1968, Johnson's last year in office, the United States had some 536,100 military personnel in Vietnam, and 30,610 military personnel had been killed in action.

Also appearing in photograph 3-10 is Dean Rusk, Johnson's secretary of state, who was one of his most trusted advisors. Johnson is said to have remarked that his greatest mistake as president was in not getting rid of all the Kennedy holdovers except Dean Rusk.

Johnson's secretary of defense for most of his tenure was Robert S. McNamara (3-11). A feature of the Johnson-McNamara Defense Department was that the civilian complement not only determined policy, which was proper, but micromanaged tactics, which was ill-advised. From the first inclined to be pessimistic, McNamara eventually lost not only the will to win but the will to fight. He resigned on February 29, 1968.

McGeorge Bundy (3-12), Johnson's National Security Advisor, had been one of Kennedy's bright young men, the type of Groton-Yale-Harvard Law School individuals with whom Johnson was not really at ease. Bundy had a brilliant mind and was not overawed by power. He was in Vietnam in February 1965 when the Vietcong attacked a U.S. installation near Pleiku, and he recommended activation of a plan for retaliatory air action against North Vietnam. Bundy had reservations about the war; he did not want a pullout, but questioned the ultimate success of a buildup. He resigned his post and on April 1, 1966, was succeeded by Dr. Walt W. Rostow.

The American presence in Vietnam briefly reached its peak (553,400 military personnel) under Richard M. Nixon (3-13) on April 30, 1969. At the end of 1973, Nixon's last full year as president, only 50 remained. Combat did not cease abruptly, however, and every engagement roused the liberal media to such a pitch that one might have supposed the war was escalating instead of winding down. On August 14, 1973, the United States officially ceased all direct military action in Vietnam, as well as in Laos and Cambodia. The ensuing year should have been one of quiet satisfaction for Nixon. In 1972, he had been reelected by a resounding majority and in 1973, active American participation in the Vietnam War had ended on his watch. Instead, he self-destructed in the sordid fiasco of Watergate.

Like Nixon, Secretary of Defense Melvin Laird (3-14) was a professional politician. He had served several terms in the House of Representatives. He possessed a well-developed sense of self-preservation and recognized in Vietnam a quicksand that could swallow him and the entire Nixon administration. Any major project is the

3-10 President of the United States Lyndon B. Johnson (right) confers with Dean Rusk, his secretary of State.

3-12 Johnson administration National Security Advisor McGeorge Bundy.

3-11 Robert S. McNamara, secretary of defense under Presidents Kennedy and Johnson.

work of many, but Laird was considered the leading spirit behind Vietnamization, a policy that he announced as early as March 1969, whereby South Vietnam would gradually take over and the United States would pull out.

On January 30, 1973, Elliott L. Richardson (3-15) replaced Laird, and in turn was replaced by James Schlesinger on July 2 of that year.

All of these men, from presidents on down, were intelligent, well-meaning, hard-working and patriotic, but they were caught in a current that no one seemed to have the skill or the will to navigate, much less control.

3-13 President Richard M. Nixon visits with U.S. troops during July 1971.

3-15 Elliott L. Richardson, Melvin Laird's successor as secretary of Defense.

3-14 Nixon administration secretary of Defense Melvin Laird answers questions from the press.

Chapter 4
America Commits to the Fight

When the French withdrew, U.S. policy toward Vietnam lost whatever dichotomy it may have had. It became simply a question of whether or not to support an Asian country trying to establish an anticommunist regime. And how far should that support go? The North Vietnamese were not idle; in July 1959 they organized a logistical group to handle the movement of men and material southward. And approximately 4,000 South Vietnamese communists who had been training in the North began moving homeward to form the cadre of the Vietcong guerrillas. Also in July, two American servicemen, a major and a master sergeant, were killed when Vietcong guerrillas struck a MAAG post in Bien Hoa, not far from Saigon—a clear indication that the Vietcong would not hesitate to provoke the United States.

In November 1960 John F. Kennedy was elected president of the United States; only a few days later a South Vietnamese military coup came close to ousting President Diem. By May 1961 the situation had deteriorated to the point where Vice President Lyndon B. Johnson visited Saigon to meet with Diem. Would Diem accept U.S. combat forces? By nature suspicious and jealous of his position, Diem was cautious; he wanted them if the North openly invaded the South, otherwise not, because he was afraid he would lose his sovereignty. By June, however, he was asking for U.S. troops to train his own soldiers.

That autumn Kennedy sent retired General Maxwell D. Taylor to Saigon to assess the situation. Reaching South Vietnam in October, he and his group soon realized that Diem's government was in trouble and that the ARVN was ineffective. He believed that the U.S. program in South Vietnam could not succeed without 6,000 to 8,000 American combat troops, but he fully recognized and reported the dangers of this policy, including escalation. He also recommended sending three

4-1 A Marine helicopter pilot airlifts South Vietnamese Army personnel during a strike against the Vietcong in May 1962.

squadrons of helicopters. Kennedy opted for a middle course, deciding against the troops but sending two companies of helicopters.

These reached South Vietnam on December 11. Five days later, specific U.S. aircraft were authorized to engage in combat missions if one of the crew was Vietnamese. By the Geneva agreements, bombers were not allowed in Indochina, so B-26s and SC-47s were officially termed "reconnaissance bombers."

The helicopters were surprisingly successful (4-1). This type of warfare was new to the Vietcong and they suffered high casualties in frantic attempts to run from the attacks. The operation had its weaknesses, however, and the Americans had to train the ARVN soldiers in fundamentals that U.S. soldiers would have learned in basic training before arriving on a battlefield (4-2). Absurdly, the helicopters used ultra high frequency (UHF) radios, the supporting fighters very high frequency (VHF). Nevertheless, the choppers proved formidable and during the first month of 1962 seemed to be turning the tide (4-3).

For some months the ARVN enjoyed some measure of success, but the Vietcong gradually gained the knack of antihelicopter defense—shooting back instead of running away—and within a year had considerably slowed the helicopters' efficiency. A search for Vietcong in a rural area depicted in photograph 4-4 resulted in four prisoners (4-5).

The U.S. military underwent several high level adjustments in 1962. On February 6, MAAG became

4-3 A South Vietnamese soldier shows the flag during operations against the Vietcong during the summer of 1962.

4-2 Vietnamese soldiers train in the field during May 1962.

4-4 A Vietnamese infantryman searches for Vietcong insurgents during June 1962.

4-5 The search is successful and nets four glum Vietcong prisoners.

4-6 President John F. Kennedy (left) looks on while Attorney General Robert F. Kennedy (right) administers the oath of office to General Maxwell D. Taylor as chairman of the Joint Chiefs of Staff on October 1, 1962. (See photograph 3-9)

MACV (U.S. Military Assistance Command Vietnam), which placed the U.S. operations in Vietnam on a higher level. On October 1, with President Kennedy's support, General Taylor became chairman of the Joint Chiefs of Staff (4-6).

The Cuban missile crisis occurred in October 1962, and for a while, until Khrushchev blinked, Vietnam received little attention. However, by December 31, U.S.

strength in Vietnam had more than tripled since 1961.

The year 1963 opened inauspiciously, with Vietcong guerrillas at Ap Bau in the Mekong Delta overwhelming a much larger ARVN force. If the latter had tried, they could not have made a worse showing. No officer above the rank of captain was present, and knowing Diem's views on casualties they were reluctant to take aggressive action. They also lost a number of men when an ARVN

4-7 An L-19 Army reconnaissance aircraft fuels at Vinh Long airstrip on February 21, 1963.

4-8 In late February 1963, a South Vietnamese soldier cleans his Thompson M-1A1 submachine gun.

4-9 American advisor 1st Lt. Joseph G. Cincotti instructs some troops in the use of map and compass prior to an exercise during March 1963.

4-10 Lt. Joe M. Clement, an advisor to the 7th ARVN Infantry Division, distributes leaflets and pictures to South Vietnamese civilians near the ARVN training area

air strike accidentally struck a friendly unit. The U.S. press exploded in anger against Diem.

The most important and spectacular events of 1963 occurred in the political arena. Out in the field, U.S. advisors and their ARVN colleagues plugged away at fundamentals, such as aerial reconnaissance (4-7). South Vietnamese soldiers familiarized themselves with their weapons (4-8). Even such ordinary items as maps and compasses were strange to the Vietnamese, and U.S. advisors provided instruction in their use (4-9). An ongoing project was to convince Vietnamese civilians that the war did indeed concern them, and to solicit their support for government forces (4-10).

At times the task of trying to make soldiers out of the South Vietnamese frustrated the Americans. These men had the same blood and background as those being molded into a disciplined, efficient army by such North Vietnamese officers as Giap. The difference was leadership and motivation (4-11).

The year 1963 saw one of the ugliest developments in the war—the Buddhist protests and Diem's repressive response. It began with what should have been a minor incident. Buddhists in Hué were forbidden to fly religious flags on May 8 in celebration of Buddha's birthday. The ban was particularly galling to the Buddhists because the local Catholics had been permitted to celebrate the birthday of their archbishop—who happened to be one of Diem's brothers. The Buddhists complained, but the apology that would have defused the situation was not forthcoming. Instead, Diem's government sent troops to quell the disorder, and in the process killed eight Buddhist monks (4-12). The protests spread; one manifestation was the suicide by burning of several Buddhist monks. The media circulated the story widely and caused a wave of revulsion worldwide, all of which had little or no effect on the military situation or on the men in the field (4-13).

The political situation became explosive, culminating in the overthrow and assassination of Diem, followed in the same month—November—by the assassination of President Kennedy.

On January 16, 1964, Washington signalled how important South Vietnam had become by sending one of America's most distinguished generals to prepare to become commander of MACV. General William C. "Westy" Westmoreland (4-14) had served with distinction in World War II and the Korean War, as an instructor at the Army War College, various staff and command assignments, and as superintendent at West Point. After a requisite six months as deputy to General Paul Harkins,

4-11 April 1963. American advisor Maj. Allan W. Galfund photographed these Vietnamese marines trudging wearily back to camp after attempting to trap a Vietcong battalion in the Plain of Reeds area, deep in the Mekong Delta region.

Westmoreland took command of MACV on June 20, 1964.

The American mission was still to train ARVN personnel. A feature of many ARVN sites was the presence of the soldiers' families, which hindered mobility and efficiency, moreover, it practically ensured such tragedies as occurred at Cai Be on July 20, 1964, when a Vietcong mortar attack killed eleven men, ten women, and thirty children.

In contrast, on February 7, 1964, President Johnson had ordered American dependents withdrawn from South Vietnam, a sure sign that the U.S. government expected the action in Vietnam to escalate. Giap was strengthening the Vietcong with improved weapons, better organization, and a steady influx of North Vietnamese. Several times the Vietcong attacked U.S. positions, but the Americans did not retaliate.

Oddly enough, it was action at sea that escalated this hang-fire situation. The U.S. Navy had been engaging in Operation DeSoto, an intelligence project to gather information on North Vietnam's radar and electronics capability, as well as hydrographic conditions. In July a certain amount of goodwill activity, such as concerts and other social events, was under way between U.S. Navy brass and the South Vietnamese (4-15 and 4-16).

The afternoon of August 2, the U.S. destroyer *Maddox* (4-17) was en route to a DeSoto mission, was in

4-12 A monument erected near downtown Hué commemorates the deaths of Buddhist monks killed by President Diem's troops in June 1963.

4-13 Strike force billets at the Vietnamese Special Forces Camp in An Diem during the summer of 1963.

4-14 President Johnson and General William C. Westmoreland in the White House Rose Garden.

international waters about 130 miles off two North Vietnamese islands. Three North Vietnamese torpedo boats attacked *Maddox*, which then was 28 miles off North Vietnam. *Maddox* retaliated, making a direct hit on a PT boat. About an hour later, F-8E fighters from the carrier *Ticonderoga* appeared, leaving a patrol boat dead in the water and damaging the remaining PT boats, which fled northward while *Maddox* took off toward the southeast (4-18, 4-19 and 4-20).

At first, Johnson decided to continue his policy of nonreprisal, and to pretend the incident had been a mistake on the part of North Vietnam. But he continued Operation DeSoto, added another destroyer, *Turner Joy*, to the patrol; U.S. aircraft carriers remained in the waters off Vietnam (4-21). Late the next day, the destroyers' radar signaled three craft approaching at high speed. This apparently was a valid sighting, but the rest of the action, on an overcast night, with crews engaged in only their first or second sea fight, was so confused that no one knows exactly what happened; some claimed that there never was a North Vietnamese attack that night.

4-15 Saigon, July 21, 1964. The Navy Band of the Republic of South Vietnam plays during welcoming ceremonies for the USS *Oklahoma City* (CLG-5), which had assumed its duties as flagship of the Seventh Fleet two weeks before. On board was Vice Adm. Roy L. Johnson, Commander-in-Chief, U.S. Seventh Fleet.

4-16 Correspondent David Horowitz of NBC News interviews Admiral Johnson, who has just arrived on his first goodwill visit to Saigon.

Nevertheless, the North Vietnamese established August 5 (August 4 in Washington) as their official Navy Day, to celebrate "our first victory over the U.S. Navy," an indication that something happened.

This time Johnson called off DeSoto temporarily, but he and the National Security Council ordered a retaliatory attack on Vinh, the North Vietnamese PT boat base (4-22 and 4-23). Considerable damage resulted, including eight of the PT boats destroyed and twenty-one damaged (4-24), at the cost of two U.S. aircraft lost and two damaged.

The Gulf of Tonkin incidents raised the level of action closer to actual war, and resulted in serious discussions in Washington and Saigon (4-25). The most important result was the approval of the Tonkin Gulf Resolution by the Congress on August 10. It did not declare war, but gave the president wide powers to use whatever force he deemed necessary to support South Vietnam and other allies in Southeast Asia and to decide when an area had attained "peace and security." At the time, public sentiment was still solidly behind the president, and the resolution sailed through Congress with

4-17 Destroyer *Maddox* (DD-731) on patrol in the Far East during 1964.

4-18 North Vietnamese Swatow gunboat under way off the coast of Vietnam, close to its top speed of 28 knots. The armament of these Chinese-made craft included depth charges and 37mm and 14.5mm guns. They also carried surface-search radar.

only two "nays" in the Senate and none in the House. That same month, presumably in retaliation for the U.S. action in the Gulf of Tonkin (4-26 and 4-27), there was a guerrilla attack on U.S. troops staying in the Caravelle Hotel in downtown Saigon.

For the American ground troops in Vietnam, these occurrences were only dim echoes of far-off events. They were concerned with their customary training and advisory missions (4-28). Early October saw South Vietnamese action against Vietcong forces at Ca Mau, the peninsula in the Mekong Delta that is the southernmost tip of Vietnam (4-29 and 4-30). At a higher command level, Westmoreland's deputy, General John L. Throckmorton, held an inspection tour of South Vietnam's River Defense Force Training Center at Thu Thiem (4-31). A grimmer reason for an inspection occurred on November 1, when Vietcong forces mounted a mortar attack on Bien Hoa Air Base, destroying five B-57s, seriously damaging eight other aircraft, killing four Americans and wounding seventy-six. This time Westmoreland and Taylor visited the site in person (4-32). The latter recommended a retaliatory air raid on North Vietnam, but

4-19 Capt. John J. Herrick (left), commander of the *Ticonderoga* during the North Vietnamese torpedo attacks on August 2 and 4, 1964. At right stands Cmdr. Herbert L. Ogier, captain of *Maddox*.

4-20 Lt. Cmdr. Dempster M. Jackson, executive officer of *Maddox*, casts an indignant scowl toward the camera as he stands beside a protruding enemy round that struck the ship's Mark 56 fire director pedestal during the North Vietnamese attack on August 2.

4-21 USS *Midway (CVA-41)* steams in the South China Sea off Vietnam during the Gulf of Tonkin crisis.

4-22 A Douglas A-4C Skyhawk catapults from an aircraft carrier during operations in the Gulf of Tonkin.

4-23 Action in the Gulf of Tonkin, August 5, 1964. A Swatow gunboat and P-4 motor torpedo boat come under attack by U.S. carrier aircraft during operation Pierce Arrow retaliatory strikes that followed attacks on *Maddox*.

predictably, Johnson declined. No way would he, the "peace candidate," authorize direct military action within days of the presidential election.

The situation in South Vietnam was deteriorating so rapidly that in late November Johnson recalled Ambassador Taylor from Saigon for conferences with Secretary of Defense McNamara in the White House on December 1 (4-33).

December saw another bombing in Saigon—an old hotel, Brinks, that had been converted to bachelor officers' quarters. Although two Americans were killed and thirty-eight wounded, Johnson once again rejected Taylor's recommendation for a retaliatory air raid. If Johnson thought this forbearance might cool things off, he was sadly mistaken, on December 28 the 9th Vietcong Division destroyed two crack ARVN units at Binh Gia. In addition, U.S. intelligence learned in December 1964 that North Vietnam had begun to send the 325th NVA Division into South Vietnam. This action changed the entire character of the war—it became an invasion of one sovereign nation by another.

Johnson, as the newly-elected president of the United

4-24 A Swatow lies dead in the water, leaking fuel, following an air strike by U.S. Navy aircraft on August 5.

4-25 American leaders who assessed the impact and implications of events in the Gulf of Tonkin—(left to right) Maxwell D. Taylor, who in June 1964 had replaced Henry Cabot Lodge as ambassador to South Vietnam; Dean C. Rusk, secretary of State; President Lyndon B. Johnson; and Robert S. McNamara, secretary of Defense.

4-26 The Caravelle Hotel in downtown Saigon.

States rather than the "peace candidate", was more inclined to consider a retaliatory policy, as urged by the Joint Chiefs of Staff (4-34). These senior military officers knew that quick, decisive action usually was not only the most effective way to meet a challenge but also in the long run the most merciful.

The next challenge was not long in coming. Early in the morning of February 7, the Vietcong attacked the American airfields at Pleiku and at nearby Camp Holloway. Eight Americans were killed and seventy-six were so badly wounded they required evacuation. Nine helicopters were put out of action and fifteen other aircraft were damaged.

This time Johnson ordered prompt reprisals. Under Operation Flaming Dart (4-35), attacks were carried out against preselected targets, in this case communist troop staging areas in North Vietnam. Johnson's Special Assistant for National Security Affairs, McGeorge Bundy, was in Vietnam at the time (4-36) and was able to give Johnson a prompt report. The initial Flaming Dart action was not a notable success. In a pattern destined to be repeated, civilian authorities in Washington (including

4-27 Vietnamese police escort an American serviceman injured in the explosion that partially destroyed the 4th, 5th, and 6th floors of the Caravelle Hotel on August 25, 1964.

4-28 Armed with an M-1 carbine, infantry advisor Capt. Don Christensen leads an ARVN machine-gun crew through a rice paddy on August 27, 1964.

4-29 4 October 1964. A South Vietnamese Ranger searches the body of a Vietcong guerrilla killed in a government operation against the communists near Ca Mau, 40 miles southwest of Saigon.

4-31 Commander Chon, River Force Commander, and Lt. Gen. John L. Throckmorton view a River Force demonstration in October 1964.

4-30 Vietcong corpses gathered for burial at Ca Mau.

4-32 General William C. Westmoreland and Ambassador Maxwell Taylor visit Bien Hoa Air Base on November 1 in the wake of a Vietcong mortar attack.

4-33 The White House, December 1, 1964. President Johnson meets with Robert McNamara and Maxwell Taylor to discuss the situation in Vietnam.

4-34 The Joint Chiefs of Staff on February 2, 1965. Seated (left to right) are Admiral David L. McDonald, CNO; General Earle G. Wheeler, Chairman; General Harold K. Johnson, Army Chief. Standing are (left to right) General John P. McConnell, Air Force Chief; General Wallace M. Greene, Commandant, USMC.

4-35 Secretary of Defense Robert McNamara briefs newsmen on February 7, 1965 concerning Operation Flaming Dart.

4-36 McGeorge Bundy, Special Assistant to President Johnson for National Security Affairs, inspects damage to American compounds in Dar Lac province on February 7 in the wake of Vietcong attacks.

Johnson) selected the targets and the force to be used, targets that were often the least productive on the list. The president often even acted as flight scheduler after assessing photographs of bomb damage.

With action escalating rapidly, General Westmoreland became concerned about the security of the airfields, particularly Da Nang. His deputy, General Throckmorton, was horrified when he checked the ARVN's security arrangements at Da Nang, and recommended that a U.S. Marine Expeditionary Brigade be sent to take over. Westmoreland reduced the request to two Marine battalions, which Johnson approved on February 26, 1965. Marines began landing at Da Nang on March 7 (4-37). Experienced in emergency operations, the Marines soon began to set up their positions (4-38). Marine units continued to arrive through the spring of 1965 (4-39). America was in the war.

On March 2, 1965, Operation Rolling Thunder, the air assault on North Vietnam that lasted through October 1968, began, changing the nature of the conflict and carrying the United States past the point of no return. No longer would air raids be simply one-for-one, tit-for-tat retaliatory strikes; this was an ongoing campaign and it was war, whether or not acknowledged as such. One objective was to pressure Hanoi to cease its support of the Vietcong, another to cut the supply routes to the South.

4-37 Marines of the 9th Marine Expeditionary Brigade splash ashore at Da Nang.

4-38 Marine defensive positions at Da Nang. Here, men of F Company, 2d Battalion, 12th Marines, man a 105mm howitzer position.

4-39 The Marine buildup continues as the men of Battalion Landing Team 2/3 hit the beach at Da Nang on April 10, 1965.

The concept was questionable. Under Secretary of State George Ball (4-40), who had warned Kennedy against committing U.S. forces to Vietnam, had been a member of the United States Strategic Bombing Survey team that assessed World War II efforts. Ball had serious doubts about the prospects of Operation Rolling Thunder having the desired effects on North Vietnam's economy and military capability. He was right. Great Britain and Germany were highly industrialized countries, yet air power alone had forced neither to its knees in World War II. Largely rural North Vietnam was even less vulnerable to air strikes, especially because the targets were severely restricted. At first targets were limited to such strictly military objectives as radar sites and barracks, making photoreconnaissance more important than ever (4-41 and 4-42). U.S. aircraft were forbidden

4-40 Under Secretary of State George W. Ball.

4-41 Two RF-101 Voodoos take off on a photoreconnaissance mission from Tan Son Nhut Air Base. Note the wreckage of an aircraft at center.

4-42 A low-flying RF-101 casts its shadow on a bombed-out bridge 15 miles north of the DMZ on April 22, 1965.

4-43 Operation Rolling Thunder begins. A Martin B-57 Canberra releases one of its bombs over North Vietnam in March 1965.

4-44 B-52 bombers, having flown 12 hours from Guam drop their loads of 750-pound and 1,000-pound bombs on July 7, 1965.

4-45 Craters made byB-52 saturation bombing on War Zone D.

4-46 Napalm/ phosphorous bombs dropped by a Vietnamese Air Force A-1E Skyraider fighter-bomber devastate a Vietcong insurgent military camp hidden in the trees south of Can Tho in Phong Dinh province.

RADAR

BAMBOO MATTING

4-47 Low-level reconnaissance photograph taken by a U.S. Air Force plane in August 1965 reveals an SA-2 surface-to-air (SAM) missile battery prepared by the North Vietnamese.

to fly north of the 19th parallel, and the most lucrative targets were beyond that line. Moreover, Johnson and McNamara, not the military, controlled the raids, which began on March 2, 1965 (4-43).

While Rolling Thunder pounded North Vietnam, American air attacks continued in the south. For instance, 540 tons of bombs fell on War Zone D, a Vietcong staging and training area 30 miles from Saigon (4-44 and 4-45). The Vietnamese Air Force was also active during this period (4-46).

Eventually, American aviators would challenge the most intense air defenses in history. Those around Hanoi and Haiphong were a fearsome cauldron of MiGs, surface-to-air missiles (SAMs), and antiaircraft guns, the latter particularly effective (4-47). It was not until July 7, 1965, that two F-4C fighter crews could claim the first MiG kills (4-48). By that time U.S. missions had been expanded, the cut-off line moved to 20°33" and such infrastructure targets as power plants, railroads, and bridges had been added to the target list. Bombing continued throughout 1965 against both North Vietnam and the Vietcong (4-49, 4-50 and 4-51).

U.S. naval air played a large part in Rolling Thunder. In fact, Admiral Ulysses S. Grant "Oley" Sharp, com-

mander-in-chief, Pacific Fleet, was officially in charge and North Vietnam was divided into U.S. Air Force and U.S. Navy bombing areas. Photograph 4-52 shows the carrier *Kitty Hawk* preparing to load planes for action. Four aircraft carriers (4-53) were an impressive sight as they executed a simultaneous turn to port in the Gulf of Tonkin in March 1965 in support of Rolling Thunder. Photograph 4-54 shows men aboard *Ranger* watching as Rolling Thunder began. Later, fire aboard *Ranger* would send it back to the West Coast for repairs. Photograph 4-55 shows a tense moment aboard the *Coral Sea* prior to launching. In April 1965 aircraft from *Coral Sea* attacked various Vietcong positions.

Such action photographs as 4-56, 4-57 and 4-58 give a picture of crisp efficiency; but in reality Rolling Thunder was so ineffective that Taylor and Westmoreland both feared that South Vietnam would collapse before the operation began to produce real results. Nor did the communists permit Rolling Thunder to go unchallenged. They stepped up their attacks in South Vietnam (4-59), and the Vietcong continued their sabotage, going so far as to attack the U.S. embassy on March 30, 1965 (4-60 and 4-61). On April 6, 1965, Johnson authorized the use of American ground troops in South Vietnam. The next

4-48 After being awarded Distinguished Flying Crosses, F-4 pilots of the 45th Tactical Fighter Squadron celebrate the first MiG kills of the Vietnam War on July 7, 1965. From the left: 1st Lt. George Larsen, Capt. Ronald C. Anderson, Capt. Kenneth D. Holcombe (partially hidden), Capt. Thomas S. Roberts, Maj. Richard Hall, Capt. Arthur C. Clark, and Capt. Wilbur Anderson.

4-49 Prior to takeoff in his F-100 fighter-bomber, 1st Lt. James D. Kempton of the 481st Tactical Fighter Squadron dons his flight suit at Tan Son Nhut Air Base in September 1965.

4-50 November 1965. Lt. Col. Gerald Beisner, Commanding Officer, 558th Tactical Fighter Squadron, prepares to climb out of the front cockpit of his F4C, while 1st Lt. Charles T. Jaglinski has already made an exit. Their squadron was equipped with the first camouflaged F-4Cs to arrive in Vietnam.

4-51 An F-100 Super Sabre drops a pair of 500-pound general purpose bombs on a Vietcong target in the Mekong Delta during air activity in late December 1965.

4-52 Crewman on board *Kitty Hawk (CVA-63)* wheel three 250-pound bombs on the flight deck during loading operations.

4-53 Four aircraft carriers from Task Force 77 and their accompanying screen.

4-54 Primary Flight Control on *Ranger*. Men observe flight operations during the kickoff of Rolling Thunder.

4-55 An A-4C on *Coral Sea (CVA-43)* awaits the signal for takeoff during late March 1965.

4-56 An F-8 Crusader fires a Zuni rocket into a Vietcong target in the South.

4-57 The universal descriptive pantomime of the fighter pilot. Cmdr. Lowell R. Myers describes his MiG-21 kill over Vinh Son while flying an F-8 Crusader.

4-58 Men standing near the Landing Signal Officer's console on *Constellation* (CVA-64) watch intently as an A-4C descends toward the flight deck. Note the lowered tail-hook

day, in a speech at Johns Hopkins University, he offered to negotiate with North Vietnam, which promptly refused. Later that month Johnson sent Secretary of Defense McNamara to see the situation for himself (4-62).

Throughout the rest of 1965, American units and personnel moved into South Vietnam (4-63 and 4-64). Nor were all the newcomers Americans. Johnson had appealed to the free world for "collective defense" in Southeast Asia. A total of 39 nations sent aid of various types, but only six—Australia, New Zealand, Thailand, the Philippines, and the Republic of Korea—sent military forces. All of these but Korea were members of the Southeast Asia Treaty Organization (SEATO). In June, Australia sent the 1st Battalion, Royal Australian Regiment, which had orders to engage in combat if necessary. McNamara made another trip to Vietnam in August, this time visiting the 3d Marine Division (4-65).

In May, the U.S. Navy commenced Operation

4-59 Medical personnel collect dead and wounded in the wake of a Vietcong attack on Bien Hoa Air Base on May 16, 1965. An A-1E Skyraider is in the background. A-1s were workhorses, often providing close air support and cover for downed pilots during rescue missions.

4-60 Secretary of Defense McNamara arrives in Vietnam in late April 1965, greeted on his arrival by his South Vietnamese counterpart, Gen. Nguyen Huu Co. U.S. Deputy Ambassador U. Alexis Johnson stands at center.

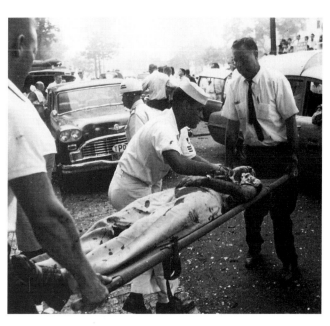

4-61 A Navy hospital corpsman lends aid to a man wounded in the March 30, 1965, attack on the U.S. embassy.

4-62 Vietnamese and American civilians lie on stretchers after sustaining injuries during the Vietcong attack on the U.S. embassy in Saigon on March 30, 1965.

4-63 Ordnance, signal, and medical specialists of the Army's 1st Logistical Command disembark from *General J. C. Breckenridge* (AP-176), boarding an LCU in preparation for the short trip into the beach area at Vung Tau on July 12, 1965.

4-64 Men clamber off the LCU at Vung Tau. A LARC-5 lies in the background at right.

4-65 While touring the 3d Marine Division operating area near Da Nang during August 1965, Secretary of Defense McNamara and General Westmoreland visit with General Thi, I Corps Commander.

Market Time, conducted by Task Force 115 out of Cam Ranh Bay, for surveillance and interdiction of the coastal waters. It continued until 1971. While most supplies reached the southern communists by land, Market Time was instrumental in virtually shutting down the sea lanes. It is claimed that in 1965 alone, U.S. sailors boarded approximately 200,000 craft. Total boardings are estimated at well over half a million over the six-year period. Few if any large cargo vessels were involved; most were small boats with very limited cargo space, a sort of seagoing Ho Chi Minh Trail operation, although not nearly so effective thanks to the U.S. Navy.

4-66 Former vice president Richard M. Nixon says good-bye to American and South Vietnamese officers before his departure from Da Nang.

4-67 Here on September 14, 1965, the 1st Cavalry Division (Airmobile) boards landing craft off Qui Nhon. The view looks down the starboard side of *Boxer* (CVA-21).

All this activity drew a number of visiting dignitaries to the major debarkation point of Da Nang, including former vice president Richard M. Nixon (4-66). While Da Nang was especially busy, it was not the only location through which American servicemen poured during the balance of 1965. For example, on September 14, the 1st Cavalry Division (Airmobile) landed at Qui Nhon to await transport by air and convoy to their tactical operations area near An Khe. This shipment included 15,800 men and 424 CH-47 Chinook helicopters (4-67).

How would even this elite division perform against battle-seasoned NVA Main Force soldiers? The answer came at Ia Drang. On November 14, the 1st Cavalry Division's helicopters brought the 7th Cavalry into the valley of Ia Drang. General Chu Huy Man, the North Vietnamese commander, promptly countered with three battalions. For a while it seemed the 7th Cavalry might be fated to replay its famous "last stand" at Little Big Horn, but they held their ground. A renewed North Vietnamese attack the next morning, November 15, resulted in intense fighting. A few hours later, U.S. firepower began to turn the tide. Artillery, fighter-bombers, and B-52s joined the gallant ground fighters to such good purpose that by the next morning General Man gave up and retreated toward Cambodia. The NVA had lost 634 known dead—probably many more—while the Americans counted 79 killed and 121 wounded.

The answer had been a resounding "Yes!"—American troops could take on the NVA veterans and win big. General Giap took this lesson very much to heart. Convinced that the NVA and Vietcong could not defeat the Americans in conventional battle without suffering such unacceptable casualties, he reasoned that the NVA should rely on guerrilla warfare and avoid major battles. It would be communist patience versus American impatience, and Giap reasoned that eventually the United States would give in.

The young Americans such as those of the 1st Cavalry had not yet been infected with the cynicism and defeatism that would come later as the war dragged on, both aimlessly and endlessly. During the early phase of involvement, these American soldiers believed strongly in their mission of protecting the South Vietnamese from the communists (4-68). The arrival of Christmas gave them a brief cause for celebration (4-69).

It had been an eventful, significant year. Nguyen Cao Ky had taken over as premier on June 11, and to everyone's surprise his government remained fairly stable, especially in comparison with the eight that had preceded him since Diem's downfall. On July 28, Johnson

announced that U.S. combat forces in Vietnam would be increased to 100,000. Less than one month later, the first engagement fought entirely by U.S. troops took place, when Marine Operation Starlight destroyed a Vietcong post near Chu Lai.

On Christmas Day, Johnson suspended Rolling Thunder in the hope that this gesture would persuade Ho Chi Minh to negotiate. Why the president believed this might succeed remains a mystery, but no doubt all concerned were glad of the respite, because in the future action would rapidly increase and the tools of war would become more plentiful and deadly.

4-68 On October 1, 1965, Sgt. W. R. Melton of the 2d Platoon, D Company, 9th Marines, talks to villagers about Vietcong activity in their area.

4-69 Soldiers representing a cross-section of their native land decorate their Christmas tree at Tan Son Nhut Air Base in the waning days of 1965. Left to right, the men are: PFC Raymond R. Schultz of Red Bluff, California; SP4 Glenn A. Rasmussen of LaGrange, Illinois; and SP5 Carlos Lopez of Brooklyn, New York.

Chapter 5
Tools of War

Just how well-equipped militarily were the North Vietnamese and the Americans for a major war? North Vietnam may have been the only modern nation to have started such a conflict without possessing a single weapon of its own manufacture. It relied principally on Russian and Chinese arms, with a few odds and ends such as American equipment the Chinese had captured in Korea. What North Vietnam did have was the one constant without which the most sophisticated weaponry is useless—men willing and able to fight and die.

The Vietcong, South Vietnamese communists, were North Vietnam's shock troops in the South. They were guerrillas, and it has been said that no one has ever devised an adequate defense against guerrilla warfare. They wore no uniforms; dressed in the same type of clothing as the local peasants, and blended into the landscape when their mission was completed.

The man portrayed in photograph 5-1 is typical. His sparse equipment includes a flimsy helmet, a small haversack to hold a cup of rice and a few magazines of ammunition, and what is either a Soviet 7.62mm Simonov SL (SKS) rifle or the Chinese Type 56 copy, which had a ten-round charger-loader magazine. Both the Soviet Union and China supplied this weapon in enormous numbers to the North Vietnamese. Other commonly used items appear in photograph 5-2, a helmet, tennis shoe, and a sandal made from a discarded tire.

In photograph 5-3 shows a Vietcong guerrilla with one of his more conventional comrades—a North Vietnamese soldier. The NVA regulars were well-trained and well-disciplined (5-4). In photograph 5-5 the weapons pictured include various explosives, Chinese RPG-7 rocket launchers, assorted Russian and Chinese long arms, and even outdated American M-1 rifles. The fact that they were captured by the Australians serves as a reminder that others aided the Americans in the conflict. Another assortment (5-6) includes an AK-47, RPG-7 and RPG-2 rocket launchers, a German Mauser, and a Chinese 7.2mm Type 56 machine gun. Still another display of captured weapons (5-7) includes rocket and mortar rounds, ammunition, grenades, rifles, and rocket launchers, as well as three stacks of Russian AK-47s or their Chinese Type 56 assault rifle copies, both of which were equipped with thirty-round magazines.

An American soldier might have found such miscellanies incongruous, but the NVA and the Vietcong made good use of them. Much of the equipment reaching North Vietnam came across the border from China, as evidenced by the Chinese markings on the 75mm artillery round casing in photograph (5-8). The canisters contain machine-gun ammunition. The presence of such Chinese and Russian equipment served as a reminder—if any were needed—that the North Vietnamese had powerful friends. U.S. policymakers were exceedingly nervous about the possibility that China or the Soviet Union or both might join the conflict.

5-1 The elusive Vietcong—North Vietnam's primary asset in the war against the South and its allies.

51

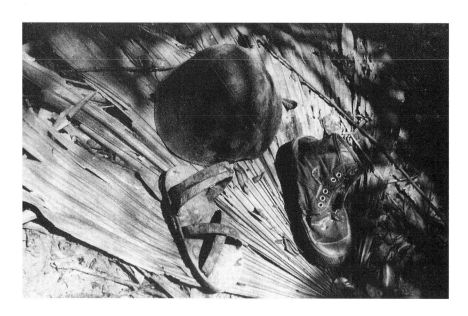

5-2 Typical Vietcong items found in a North Vietnamese base camp.

5-3 A North Vietnamese soldier (left) and a Vietcong guerrilla dig in at a bunker position.

5-4 North Vietnamese Army regulars on parade in Hanoi during the 1960s.

5-5 This cache of Vietcong/
North Vietnamese weapons
captured by the 2d Battalion,
Royal Australian Regiment
during February 1968 illustrates
the wide range of weapons
used by the communist forces.

5-6 Vietcong small arms
displayed at a defensive
position near Lai Khe
on January 8, 1968.

5-7 Captured weapons
seized during fighting near
Tan Son Nhut Air Base in
Saigon in May 1968.

5-8 U.S. forces operating just off the coast of Vietnam recovered these supplies from a gun-running trawler.

5-9 Entrance to a Vietcong tunnel complex.

5-10 View of a bamboo punji pit, designed to injure the ankle rather than to puncture the sole of the foot.

5-11 A bamboo whip, designed to be released by a trip wire.

5-12 A death fall improvised from a 55-gallon oil drum.

5-13 The Vietcong used a variety of everyday objects—in this case, a book—to make booby traps.

5-14 These empty drink cans were filled with grenades.

5-15 A Soviet-built T54 tank sits along highway QL-9 after ARVN forces immobilized it in 1972.

The Vietcong were masters of camouflage and improvisation. Photograph 5-9 shows a tunnel typical of the many hundreds of tunnels that led to underground installations. Booby traps of all kinds were a Vietcong specialty (5-10 to 5-13); even discarded trash from American garbage heaps provided raw material for booby traps (5-14).

At the other end of the armament scale, China and the Soviet Union provided heavy military hardware such as tanks (5-15), generally reserved for the NVA. The efficacy of the tanks was questionable, because the terrain of Vietnam was ill-suited for tank warfare. Roads were so primitive that tanks had to proceed in single file. If one broke down, the column was held up, possibly for hours, and the terrain off the road was frequently jungle or water-softened soil.

Virtually all of the frontline fighter strength of the North Vietnamese Air Force came from the Soviet Union. First were outdated MiG-17s (5-16), then by 1966 up-to-date fighters such as the MiG-21 began to appear.

5-16 A Mikoyan-Gurevich MiG-17, similar to those used by the North Vietnamese Air Force.

5-17 The American infantryman was the mainstay of the allied military effort to maintain the independence of South Vietnam.

5-18 A soldier clutched his M-14 rifle during a search-and-destroy mission near Bien Hoa in October 1965. Note the two magazines taped together.

5-19 PFC Michael J. Mendoza fires his M-16A1 rifle during Operation Cook in Quang Ngai province.

5-20 A Marine sniper attached to the 4th Marine Headquarters Company aims at a target through his 3x9 scope mounted on a 30.06 sniper rifle.

The backbone of the allied effort was the U.S. infantryman (5-17), whose principal weapon during the early days of the war was the M-14 rifle, successor to the venerable M-1. Although it was being replaced by the M-16 by 1965, the M-14's (5-18), ruggedness made it well suited for the wet, immoderate Vietnamese climate. The M-16A1 (5-19) fired 5.56mm ammunition, and though much lighter and more compact than the M-14, the M-16's tendency to foul and jam hindered its effectiveness. The cynical quip, "don't worry: as long as you don't get wet, you'll be OK," was an indicator of the fastidious upkeep required for both rifle and ammunition. The rifle's spring-loaded magazines corroded quickly in bandoliers that were almost always wet.

Photograph 5-20 shows a Marine sniper and his 30.06 sniper rifle.

The instruction of newcomers in various techniques was a never-ending task (5-21), and unsuspecting fresh arrivals were often stuck carrying uncomfortably heavy equipment. Designed along the lines of the famous German MG-42 from World War II, the M-60 (5-22) was the Army's standard light machine gun, replacing its Browning predecessor in the early 1960s. Chief drawbacks included a tendency to overheat, a flimsy, awkward carrying handle, and its weight—nearly 24 pounds. The weapon was usually palmed off on a unit's newcomers (rarely to fire, just to carry). Radios were another hefty item often foisted on the hapless greenhorns.

The M-79 grenade launcher (5-23) was a single-shot weapon that could fire high-explosive and smoke rounds up to a maximum effective range of 150 meters. The launcher seemed to be a psychological favorite with the troops, many of whom felt keenly the isolation and exposure of the outlying firebases.

The flamethrower was a weapon of terrifying efficiency. Photograph 5-24 shows a training demonstration at Lai Khe, north of Saigon. A former Michelin rubber plantation, Lai Khe was the site of a large U.S. installation.

The M-19 81mm illustrated in 5-25 could lob mortar shells to a maximum range of 1,790 meters at a sustained rate of eighteen rounds per minute. The U.S. Army's standard medium mortar was the M-30 4.2" (5-26), which had a maximum range of over 5,000 meters and could be fired at a sustained rate of four rounds per minute, although often this was exceeded.

A variety of equipment is shown in photograph 5-27, while in 5-28 the 1st Cavalry Division (Airmobile) demonstrates the M-114 howitzer near An Khe. A holdover from World War II and Korea, the 155mm

5-21 SSgt. Herbert Suloff demonstrates grenade-throwing techniques for newly arrived troops of the 9th Infantry Division.

5-22 A soldier at Fire Base Abby fires an M-60 general purpose machine gun on January 27, 1970.

5-23 SP4 Donald Krug prepares to fire his M-79 40mm grenade launcher at an outpost on the outskirts of Saigon in December 1968.

howitzer was still the workhorse of American artillery units during the Vietnam War. It had a maximum range of nearly 14,600 meters.

The M-48A3 (5-29) was the main U.S. battle tank in Vietnam. The A3 variant had a diesel engine that greatly enhanced the vehicle's operating range and, especially important in Southeast Asia, it could ford streams up to 4 feet deep.

Another tank was the M-551 (5-30). It had a higher road speed and greater range (45 mph/34,898 lbs.) than the heavier M-48A3 (30 mph/104,000 lbs.). Accordingly, the M-551 was also used as an air-droppable assault vehicle.

A versatile asset was the M-113 armored personnel carrier (5-31), the first armored fighting vehicle of aluminum construction. By 1964, the diesel-powered M-113A1 variant was in production. The vehicle had a crew of two, and could carry eleven fully armed and equipped troops. It was used in a multitude of configurations and roles, including medical evacuation, and was fully amphibious, its track propelling it forward in the water.

Another highly mobile item was the M-109A1 self-propelled 155mm howitzer (5-32) which carried a crew of six. Photograph 5-33 displays a .50-caliber machine-gun mount at Pleiku, a town in the Central Highlands that was a communications center and the site of a large U.S. air base.

A variety of LARC (Landing Amphibious Resupply Cargo) vehicles, doubling as lighters, supported amphibious resupply operations. In photograph 5-34 a LARC picks up a load of gasoline from a refueling tanker anchored offshore. Photograph 5-35 shows a river patrol craft preparing to disembark a squad from the 16th Infantry in Gia Dinh, the province surrounding Saigon. These men were preparing to conduct a patrol seeking Vietcong in that area.

The war in Vietnam witnessed the twilight of propeller-driven, fixed-wing combat aviation, such as the T-28B fighter-bomber (5-36). Even a number of World War II-period aircraft saw action as late as the 1960s.

While U.S. Navy aircraft carriers supplemented air attacks on targets in North Vietnam, the brunt of the southern action in the South was borne by the U.S. Air Force and Marines. Photograph 5-37 shows an O-1 observation aircraft preparing to fly a forward air control mission in support of Operation Cedar Falls. Photographs 5-38 to 5-40 show three types of U.S. Air Force planes in use in Vietnam. There was also a Marine air presence at Da Nang (5-41), a city second in importance only to Saigon, and site of a major U.S. air base.

5-24 A soldier demonstrates the use of an M-7 flamethrower during a Combat Indoctrination Course at Lai Khe.

5-25 During Operation Somerset Plain in August 1968, men of the 101st Airborne Division set up their M-19 81mm mortar on Landing Zone Tabat.

5-26 Members of the 505th Infantry, 82d Airborne Division, fire a round from their M-30 4.2-inch mortar at Fire Support Base Harrison.

The South Vietnamese Air Force also participated in the air war (5-42). The war in Vietnam saw the last offensive use of a variety of aging, second-line jets, such as the B-57 shown in photograph 5-43.

B-52 bombers were stationed in Guam, where their range and air refueling permitted them to fly 12-hour round-trip missions to South Vietnam (5-44). At that time, the B-52 could carry a total of twenty-four 500-pound and 750-pound bombs externally and twenty-seven internally, nearly equal to the bombload of an entire squadron of B-17s during World War II.

In the North, Rolling Thunder air attacks, while they inflicted considerable damage, were strategically ineffective because the airmen were permitted to bomb only comparatively unproductive targets, all south of the 19th parallel. F-100 Super Sabres (5-45) were used in a ground-support role in the South. Although F-105s (5-46) did indeed score the first MiG kills over Vietnam, they served primarily as fighter-bombers in the North, particularly after the first F-4C Phantoms (5-47) arrived. All of these fighter aircraft could combat North Vietnamese fighters when challenged.

Various other aircraft and missiles, illustrated in photographs 5-48 to 5-51 saw service in Vietnam. Photograph 5-52 shows an air-to-ground U.S. Navy Bullpup missile while a Shrike air-to-ground missile appears in 5-53. The aircraft carrier *Ranger* delivered bombs and rockets (5-54). The Walleye glide bomb was first used during the Vietnam War (5-55).

Probably the most useful item in the ground force's inventory and the most popular with the men, was the helicopter. The AH-1G Cobra (5-56) escorted troop-carrying helicopters and had firepower to interdict enemy forces. The South Vietnamese military likewise relied heavily on rotary-wing air power (5-57). Photograph 5-58 provides a close look at the UH-1D "Huey" with an XM-21 weapons system.

More routine were the missions of the CH-54A (5-59), CH-47 (5-60) and H-21 (5-61) cargo helicopters. Of all the choppers, the HH-53B (5-62) rescue helicopter was the most welcome sight to downed airmen, whether they were in North Vietnam or enemy-controlled territory in South Vietnam.

From the foregoing, it is evident that the quantity and quality of U.S. matériel was vastly superior to that of the North Vietnamese. In 1965, however, Hanoi's forces seemed to be holding their own. It remained to be seen whether this situation would continue after the United States escalated its commitment to the war, or whether more and better ordnance would spell the difference.

5-27 Fragmentation hand grenades, claymore mines, and red and white flares belonging to a reconnaissance platoon of the 101st Airborne Division.

5-28 A gun crew of the 1st Cavalry Division (Airmobile) fires their M-114 155mm howitzer northeast of An Khe in Binh Dinh province.

5-29 An American M-48A3 medium tank. Note the xenon searchlight. During road-clearing operations, a mine explosion blew off its tracks.

5-30 4th Cavalry M-551
Sheridan light tanks from
the 25th Infantry Division at Cu Chi.

5-31 An M-113 armored
personnel carrier of the
4th Infantry Division moves
through the jungles of
Vietnam during June 1969.

5-32 M-109A1 self-propelled
155mm howitzer at Fire Support
Base Washington near Cu Chi.

5-33 Quadruple .50-caliber machine-gun mounted on a 2-1/2-ton truck being test-fired at Pleiku during August 1967.

5-34 A LARC of the 1st Logistical Command backs into the surf at Duc Pho.

5-35 An Army RPC (River Patrol Craft) noses onto the shore in Gia Dinh province.

5-36 T-28B fighter-bombers on the flight line at Bien Hoa Air Base.

5-37 A U.S. Air Force O-1 Bird Dog observation aircraft taxies out to the runway at Lai Khe.

5-38 In the dusk of early evening an AC-47 fires at a ground target. This type of aircraft is the famous "Puff the Magic Dragon." Note the tracer at lower right.

5-39 Ground crews direct U.S. Air Force A-1E Skyraiders from their parking areas at Pleiku in November 1966.

5-40 An excellent three-quarter view of an OV-10 Bronco in flight over Southeast Asia during the last days of December 1968. The Bronco was used for reconnaissance and to direct air attacks, but it was also armed with guns and rockets to attack ground targets.

5-41 At Da Nang Air Base, a U.S. Marine A-6 attack aircraft stands ready for takeoff on April 8, 1969.

5-42 The A-37 Dragonfly provided the South Vietnamese Air Force with much of its offensive punch in the last years of the war.

5-43 A camouflaged Martin B-57 Canberra bomber parked at Tan Son Nhut Air Base near Saigon in May 1967.

5-44 A B-52 bomber takes off from its base in Guam to attack Vietcong targets during Operation Rolling Thunder in August 1965.

5-45 F-100 Super Sabre fighters with the 90th Tactical Fighter Squadron at Bien Hoa.

5-46 Its bomb load shackled in place, this F-105 Thunderchief stands ready for action on November 14, 1965.

5-47 Crews guide a USAF F-4C Phantom out of its revetment at Cam Ranh Bay in June 1967.

5-48 Fitted with a variety of camera equipment, the F-101 Voodoo served well in its tactical reconnaissance role.

5-49 A Lockheed C-130 transport at an air base in Southeast Asia.

5-50 Two Sidewinder air-to-air heat-seeking missiles mounted under the wing of an F-105 fighter-bomber.

5-51 A2C William B. Brotton and SSgt. Raymond R. Janek load a Sparrow air-to-air radar-homing missile onto an F-4C of the 555th Tactical Fighter Squadron.

5-52 Naval ordnance personnel board an aircraft carrier hoist a Bullpup air-to-ground missile onto an A-4 Skylark. The missile carried a 1,000 pound payload.

5-53 A Shrike air-to-ground missile undergoes testing with the Navy during 1963.

5-54 Bombs and rockets arrive from the magazine of the aircraft carrier *Ranger (CVA-64)* off Southeast Asia.

5-55 The Navy's Walleye glide bomb was guided by television cameras.

5-56 The AH-1G Cobra attack helicopter was the mainstay of the U.S. Army's aerial offensive capability.

5-57 A U.S. Navy UH-1D in the Binh Thuy area.

5-58 Front view of the XM-21 weapon system mounted on a UH-1D helicopter. The pack consisted of a seven-round rocket pod and an M-134 high-rate machine gun.

5-59 A CH-54A Flying Crane with cargo pod removed sits on the landing pad at Khe San where it served the 1st Cavalry Division (Airmobile).

5-60 A CH-47 Chinook helicopter prepares to leave after disgorging its cargo of men and supplies in the Cay Giep mountains.

5-61 An H-21 light cargo helicopter during airlift operations in the vicinity of Ap Truang Hoa, 70 miles southwest of Saigon. Note the crew chief at the door observing the ground below for enemy fire.

5-62 With its 7.62mm miniguns for defense, the HH-53B Super Jolly Green Giant helicopter was used effectively in rescue and recovery operations over both South and North Vietnam.

Chapter 6
Escalation

The year 1966 opened with little cause for the Americans to be hopeful. The bombing pause—predictably—had brought no offer to negotiate from Hanoi; on the contrary, the NVA had increased the number of regiments in the South from five in mid-1965 to twelve at year's end. On January 15 South Vietnamese premier Ky met in Saigon with Ambassador Henry Cabot Lodge, Secretary of State Dean Rusk (6-1) and W. Averell Harriman, U.S. Ambassador-at-Large (not shown). Although nothing reassuring emerged from this conference, Johnson was psychologically committed to continuing aid, and on January 19 he requested Congress to approve an additional $12.8 billion to finance the war in Vietnam.

On January 25, a major search-and-destroy mission began that, under various names, lasted until March 6 (6-2 and 6-3). Originally called Operation Masher, Johnson, ever sensitive to public opinion, soon changed its name lest it provoke adverse public reaction. Most operation names were either innocuous or somewhat inspirational, whereas "Masher" had an ugly slang mean-

ing. A series of similar operations under other names followed, ending in late October. It is estimated that a total of about 3,000 NVA and Vietcong forces were killed, about ten men per day. This was an unimpressive statistic; as NVA/Vietcong losses would probably have been about the same without these operations.

Vietnam was singularly ill-suited for this type of operation. The usual blueprint for a search-and-destroy mission was to obtain intelligence—which might or might not be reliable (6-4). According to the level of enemy activity or presence reported, the Americans sent off what they considered an appropriate unit—anywhere from a platoon to a battalion—to locate the Vietcong or NVA positions Then an air and/or artillery strike was launched to prepare the way for the helicopters to land with additional troops (6-5). Sometimes the effort netted results (6-6); more often it did not.

Such missions were often ineffective because at the slightest hint of American activity the communist forces slipped away into the jungle or countryside. Even large

6-1 American officials and diplomats meet with South Vietnamese Prime Minister Nguyen Cao Ky during January 15, 1966. Pictured (left to right) are: Prime Minister Ky; Dean Rusk, U.S. secretary of State; and Henry Cabot Lodge, U.S. ambassador.

6-2 January 25, 1966. Artillery troops of the 1st Cavalry Division (Airmobile) deploy their howitzers near Bong Son during Operation Masher. Note the CH-47 Chinook helicopters.

NVA units were dispersed in small, mobile groups that changed position so frequently that intelligence was outdated almost before it was received. Then, too, Vietcong forces often refused battle, allowing quite large bases to be taken because they knew that in a few days the Americans would pull out. It was a frustrating situation for the Americans whose idea of war did not include chasing will-o'-the-wisps. In addition, the soldiers could never really relax; even men on rest leave were on 30-minute alert (6-7) and platoons were active almost daily (6-8).

Meanwhile, from February 6 to 8, Johnson convened a top-level conference in Honolulu concerning the Vietnam situation. The conference did not have a firm agenda, however, and it has been suggested that Johnson's motive was to distract attention from the televised Senate Foreign Relations Committee hearings under William J. Fulbright, which had begun on February 4. The con-

6-3 PFC George J. Pignatore, a medic with the 7th Cavalry, holds a compress gingerly against his chest, having been wounded during Operation Masher on January 25.

6-4 Terrified civilians in Bong Son undergo questioning by troops of the 1st Cavalry Division (Airmobile). At the time, troops were detaining large numbers of suspected Vietcong.

6-5 A CH-47 Chinook disgorges a portion of the 1st Cavalry Division's 3d Brigade into a secured landing zone on a mountain ridge during the first week of January 1966.

6-6 Finally cornering a number of Vietcong guerrillas after three days of operations, soldiers of the 7th Cavalry fire into a Vietcong bunker near Bong Son.

6-7 Ten days into Operation Masher, PFC Lee A. Bilbrey finally gets a bath and a "helmet shower" after his unit was relieved from operations.

6-8 Radio operator PFC Ira B. Rolston sounds the call from a Vietcong bugle (captured during the Ia Drang Valley fight) for his platoon to advance down the mountain toward their valley objective during Operation Masher.

6-9 President Johnson and Premier Ky talk informally during a conference of American and South Vietnamese leaders held in Honolulu during February 1966. President Thieu is seated on Johnson's left, while Admiral U.S. Grant Sharp sits across the table, facing the president.

ference was heavily loaded with Americans, including Johnson, McNamara, Rusk, Lodge, Westmoreland, Admiral Sharp, and General Earle Wheeler, chairman of the Joint Chiefs of Staff. Only three top Vietnamese attended—Premier Ky, President Thieu, and Defense Minister General Nguyen Huu Co (6-9).

One might have expected this conference to concentrate on the immediate strategic problem of how to win the war; instead, it devoted its main energy emphasizing the so-called pacification program, which was intended to improve the lot of the rural South Vietnamese so they would not be tempted to defect, and to secure their support against the Vietcong who needed their cooperation for success. This reflected Johnson's interest in social reform and Ky was smart enough to agree. Westmoreland was fortunate to secure a mission directive that, among other things, authorized him to order continuance of the search-and-destroy program, for which he would be severely criticized in the future. And in South Vietnam the fighting went on (6-10).

On April 1, 1966, Vietcong guerrillas positioned a vehicle in front of the Victoria Hotel in Saigon, in use as a bachelor officers' quarters for Americans. They abandoned the car and set off 200 pounds of explosives, resulting in heavy damage to the ground, second and third

6-10 Crew Chief SP4 James M. Ralph of the 229th Helicopter Assault Battalion fires his M-60 machine gun into a Vietcong position marked minutes earlier by a red smoke grenade, on March 16, 1966.

floors. Three American military police (MPs) and three civilians were killed; sixty-seven were wounded (6-11). Such incidents intensified American efforts to clear Vietcong from the area surrounding Saigon (6-12).

Apparently intoxicated by Johnson's cordiality toward him in Honolulu, Ky embarked on a series of political moves as bizarre as they were foolish, leading to riots and demonstrations, many led by Buddhists. Finally, on April 1, President Thieu called for a national political conference, to include Buddhists, and two days later promised elections for an assembly to take place in three to six months. Tri Quang, the Buddhist leader, called his people to return to order (6-13). Nevertheless, there followed months of political disorder that sidetracked the war effort as rival ARVN factions battled each other more enthusiastically than they did the Vietcong.

The promised elections took place on September 11, 1966. Government officials seemed bored by the exercise, and the Buddhists, who had demonstrated for elections but still distrusted the Catholic-dominated government of South Vietnam, threatened to boycott the proceedings. Still, an amazing number of citizens registered, estimated at two-thirds of South Vietnam's adults. Of these, 81 percent actually voted—a percentage that would have been phenomenal in an American election (6-14 and 6-15).

6-11 Confusion reigns in Saigon after the Victoria Hotel was bombed on April 1, 1966.

6-12 PFC Frederick Culp of the 1st Infantry Division holds his weapon above water while crossing a river during a search-and-destroy mission east of Saigon, near Long Tranh, in the wake of the Victoria Hotel bombing.

6-13 On April 14, 1966, Buddhists move away from a temple to begin a parade through the city in celebration of the government's decision to permit free elections in the near future.

By this time, sizable NVA forces were operating in the demilitarized zone (DMZ), including three battalions of the 324B Division. In Operation Prairie, Marines of the 3d Division swept through the Con Thien/Gio Linh area of the DMZ (6-16, 6-17 and 6-18). The operation ended on January 31, 1967, with 1,397 known NVA casualties.

A number of other army, as well as at least a dozen Marine operations, were going on throughout late 1966, including Operation Attleboro in Tay Ninh province.

6-14 September 11, 1966. The South Vietnamese vote to elect an assembly to draw up a constitution for their country. Here, President Thieu departs after voting at the polls in the City Hall in downtown Saigon.

6-15 A Vietnamese policeman and soldier monitor activity at the entry to a polling place located at a primary school in Saigon.

6-16 Lance Cpl. Charles Hill assists Sgt. Lee Jankes as he fires his M-60 machine gun at North Vietnamese troops on Hill Hui-Cray-Tre during Operation Prairie near the DMZ on 30 September 1966.

6-17 Marines of the 3d Division approach a church while on patrol during Operation Prairie near the DMZ on October 27.

6-18 Troops of M Company, 3d Battalion, 3d Marines, embark on board a CH-46 Sea Knight after making a sweep through the DMZ during Operation Prairie.

6-19 President Johnson visits Vietnam. He, General Westmoreland, and President Thieu pay their respects during the playing of the Vietnamese National Anthem on October 26, 1966.

This operation concluded on November 24, the largest U.S. operation of the war at that time. During October 1966 the U.S. Navy began Operation Sea Dragon, the interdiction of enemy supply vessels off the coast of North Vietnam, as opposed to Market Time, which had operated off South Vietnam. Sea Dragon terminated in March 1968.

In October 1966, Johnson went to Manila for another conference. On October 20, he flew to Cam Ranh Bay, much to the surprise of U.S. troops (6-19).

Throughout 1966, U.S. troops poured into South Vietnam; by the end of the year, they numbered 385,300. As of December 31, a total of 6,644 U.S. military personnel had been killed in action.

A major operation in early 1967 was Cedar Falls, conducted from January 8 to 26 in the so-called Iron Triangle, a communist base in Binh Duong province. This was near the Cambodian border, which provided an escape route for Vietcong forces. ARVN units joined the U.S. 1st and 25th Infantry Divisions, 173d Airborne Brigade, and 11th Armored Cavalry (6-20 and 6-21). Westmoreland was sure that the communists would fight to secure such bases, which were so essential to their operations, but the Vietcong continued to refuse battle. Their fighting men were more important than the installations, which could be—and were—reconstituted in a remarkably short time, despite exceedingly heavy damage to the area.

6-20 Men of the 1st Infantry Division exit a CH-47 Chinook helicopter, climbing down a rope ladder on January 8, 1967, the first day of Operation Cedar Falls, the first allied corps-sized offensive effort of 1967.

6-21 A soldier's grimace during his 100-foot descent from a CH-47 testifies to the difficulty of that task.

Westmoreland launched a similar, but larger, operation, Junction City, on February 22 using twenty-two U.S. Army and four ARVN battalions. Taking place in Tay Ninh and surrounding provinces (6-22 and 6-23), Junction City repeated the Cedar Falls pattern—Vietcong withdrawal and subsequent return as soon as U.S. and ARVN forces left the area.

Nevertheless, it would be a mistake to write off such operations as Cedar Falls and Junction City as unmitigated failures. The North Vietnamese took them very seriously. Giap for one considered them "disasters." The Americans had the initiative and had forced the Vietcong and the NVA to move main force units ever farther from populated areas. This limited their support for the local guerrillas, with a dampening effect on their morale.

A number of operations with such names as Sam Houston, Palm Beach, Pershing, Francis Marion, and Oregon took place in 1967. Operation Oregon, a search-and-destroy mission in the Duc Pho District of Quang Tri province, that included amphibious components. Photographs 6-24 through 6-29 give a picture of day-to-day action in Operation Oregon.

Operation Baker was a follow-up to Operation Oregon in Quang Tri province, this time north of Duc Pho (6-30). The immediate objective of the operation was to clear the area east of Highway 1 ("The Street

6-22 Operation Junction City, late February 1967. Troops in an M-113 armored personnel carrier stop at a bridge in Tay Ninh Province.

6-23 PFC Craig Yockey from Fresno, California, of the 5th Cavalry, uses his time off during Operation Junction City to make friends with Davey Detail, the unit's mascot.

6-24 Members of the 101st Airborne Division wait to unload their vehicles from LST-178 on May 2, 1967, during Operation Oregon.

6-25 Airborne troops trudge onto the sand near Duc Pho, commencing Operation Oregon. Note the variety of equipment and armament carried, including the M-16 rifle and M-60 machine gun.

6-26 Inland and west of Duc Pho, a UH-1B helicopter lifts men from a platoon of the 1st Cavalry Division (Airmobile) into an area where a suspected Vietcong outpost is located.

6-27 Men of Troop B, 1st Reconnaissance Squadron, 9th Cavalry, 1st Cavalry Division (Airmobile), during Operation Oregon. One points in the direction of a supposed suspected Vietcong position. Smoke canisters hang from the radio carried by the soldier at left. These were used to mark troop positions during air attacks and helicopter extractions.

Without Joy") of suspected elements of the North Vietnamese Army. Photograph 6-30 and the others in this sequence (as well as those from Operation Oregon) were taken by U.S. Army photographer SSgt. Howard C. Breedlove, whose byline appears on hundreds of Signal Corps images documenting the endless train of search-and-destroy missions from 1966 to 1967.

Air strikes preceded the infantry, but often were less than surgical in nature and produced only ambiguous results. So troops proceeded with due caution (6-31 through 6-34).

Another of the many operations of 1967 was Cochise. During its opening day, August 11, artillery fired more than 1,000 rounds into Vietcong positions (6-35).

During 1967, the U.S. Army continued its buildup of installations throughout the South, making frequent use of Vietnam's vast river system. Photograph 6-36, shows a river patrol craft and monitor, both elements of the River Assault Group of the 1099th Transportation Company, 1st Logistical Command, providing protection on August 31. With cargo safely delivered, a soldier played a tune on his harmonica (6-37).

With ever-increasing stakes and mounting casualties, members of the Johnson administration made frequent visits to inspect the continuing operations in Vietnam and to raise morale (6-38). Such visits were meant to convince the troops that somebody cared—a task that would become more and more difficult as opposition to the war increased at home.

As the year drew to an end, some operations began, some ended. American forces prepared to intercept boats that frequently carried enemy arms, equipment, and personnel on inland waterways (6-39).

In the meantime, what of the war in the air? Johnson reinstated Rolling Thunder on January 31, 1966, and bombing of North Vietnam resumed. Air-to-air combat—where individual pilots pitted their skill and courage against one another—was frequent. A disquieting new feature of these encounters was the appearance of a front-line Soviet fighter aircraft—the MiG-21. The first MiG-21 to fall to U.S. crews was shot down on August 26, 1966, by Maj. Paul J. Gilmore and 1st Lt. William T. Smith (6-40).

On June 29, 1966, Johnson ordered bombing of oil depots located near Hanoi and Haiphong. The U.S. Air Force promptly took advantage of this authority, as these bombings became increasingly controversial. The original United States Information Agency caption on photograph 6-41 states emphatically that "all bombs fell in the target area," revealing a heightened sensitivity to

6-28 Members of a reconnaissance platoon observe the results of concentrated artillery fire on a suspected enemy position west of Duc Pho.

6-29 During Operation Oregon, soldiers from the 25th Infantry Division question a group of passive villagers about Vietcong that are suspected to be in the vicinity.

charges that bombing attacks were killing large numbers of innocent civilians.

U.S. Air Force colonel James Jabra, second ranking ace of the Korean War with fifteen kills, was in Vietnam on temporary duty for only a week following a plane-ferrying mission when his three-man flight from the 418th Tactical Fighter Squadron was credited with damaging six Vietcong buildings during an air strike on a Vietcong camp (6-42).

The Americans had a healthy respect for the capabilities of MiGs (6-43) and destruction of a MiG was always a matter of pride and satisfaction (6-44). Such air activity aroused a certain nostalgia. Gregory "Pappy" Boyington, a Marine ace in World War II, visited the 1st Marine Air Wing Headquarters on August 28, 1966, giving his old squadron a chance to touch its past (6-45).

Photograph 6-46 gives a graphic picture of a bomb explosion seen from the air. Dark smoke rises from the storage area at lower right, while white smoke billows from the barracks at upper right. The buildings to the left of the smoke are part of an ammunition storage facility. The results of another F-105 strike appear in photograph 6-47.

The years 1966 and 1967 saw intensification of the air war and an accompanying increase in air-to-air encounters. As the victory tallies of the U.S. Air Force, Navy and Marine tactical fighter squadrons began to rise, there seemed a real possibility that many pilots might emerge

6-30 Men of the 25th Infantry Division wade across a shallow stream during Operation Baker on June 10, 1967. This and the next four photos were taken by SSgt. Howard C. Breedlove, who accompanied the troops on the operation.

6-31 Troops advance cautiously through a bombed-out village in Quang Tri province during Operation Baker.

6-33 2d Lt. Michael J. Pulaski (3d Platoon leader, Company A, 2d Battalion, 35th Infantry, 3d Brigade, 25th Infantry Division) briefs his squad leaders on the patrol routes they will take during their search for communist forces.

from the war as aces.* However, the North Vietnamese pilots, losing heavily to the Americans, increasingly refused combat, so the scoring binges of 1966 and 1967 tapered off. Five Americans became aces: three Air Force, two Navy. The highest scoring pilot of the period of the late 1960s was Col. Robin Olds, commanding officer of the 8th Tactical Fighter Wing (6-48). In three separate missions, Olds shot down four aircraft—one MiG-21 on January 2, 1967, another MiG-21 four months later on May 4, 1967, and a rare double kill of two MiG-17s on May 20. One of Old's many aircraft, F-4C 64-0829—flown on the May 20 mission—is on display at the U. S. Air Force Museum in Dayton, Ohio.

Another veteran of World War II who distinguished himself in Vietnam was Maj. William J. Bailey (6-49). On June 3, 1967, Maj. Ralph L. Kuster encountered a MiG after a successful strike against a ground target. The enemy pilot cut his throttle in an effort to shake the F-105, but Kuster sent the MiG flaming to the ground shortly thereafter (6-50).

Photograph 6-51 shows an F-100 firing rockets into a Vietcong position during the summer of 1967. All air action did not end with a solidly satisfactory "mission accomplished." North Vietnamese hospitality left much to be desired, and capture was every pilot's worst nightmare, considerably beyond death, which they faced daily with either the resignation of experience or the disbelief of youth. Sometimes North Vietnamese MiGs or anti-

6-32 PFC Harlan Slusser leaves a suspected enemy bunker after completing his search during Operation Baker.

---

*Five confirmed shoot-downs were necessary for a pilot to be an ace.

6-34 Lieutenant Pulaski's platoon moves out and advances over a dry rice paddy.

6-35 A Sea Stallion helicopter from Marine Heavy Helicopter Squadron 463 brings an emergency resupply of 105mm howitzer ammunition for the guns of the 11th Marines.

6-36 On August 31, 1967, a river patrol craft on the right and a monitor on the left protect a construction "convoy" as it travels down the Song Vam Co Tay River to Tan An.

6-38 Vice President Hubert Humphrey, General Westmoreland, and Lt. Gen. Robert E. Cushman, Marine commander in Vietnam, salute the men of the 3d Marine Division during ceremonies and presentation of decorations on November 1, 1967.

6-37 With construction supplies unloaded from the river boat, a soldier takes time out to relax with his harmonica.

6-39 Operation Bang Dong, November 21, 1967. Members of the 7th Infantry, 199th Light Infantry Brigade, prepare to search boats that were traveling down a wide canal.

aircraft guns resulted in a capture, to the delight of the locals (6-52). The injured received no consideration or sympathy (6-53 and 6-54).

At times a prisoner broke and aided his captors with a propaganda interview on film, which the North Vietnamese provided to foreign news correspondents (6-55). These men were not heroes, but they were not entirely contemptible; anyone who had undergone North Vietnamese grillings might well confess to anything he could think of to stop the pain and hope that his comrades would understand.

The Vietnamese conflict was not a naval war in the traditional sense, so there were no spectacular sea battles. Much of the action consisted of shelling shore installations (6-56, 6-57 and 6-58). However, carrier aircraft continued to bomb and interdict targets in North Vietnam, which cost the United States the lives of many men. Naval aviators held prisoner in the infamous Hanoi Hilton included future senator John McCain of Arizona.

As the war progressed, more and more Americans embarked on a new, dangerous experience in a land of jungles, no front lines, dysentery, and frustration—a very strange land indeed.

6-40 Maj. Paul J. Gilmore (left) and 1st Lt. William T. Smith (right) of the 480th Tactical Fighter Squadron pose for an air force photographer in front of F-4C 64-0752 on the occasion of their being the first U.S. Air Force crews to shoot down a MiG-21. Note the victory star over Smith's head.

6-41 Hanoi, June 29, 1966. Oil storage facilities go up in flames in the wake of an American bombing attack.

6-42 An air hero of two wars—Korea and Vietnam—Col. James Jabra prepares a postflight report documenting his fighter-bombing mission over Vietnam on July 18, 1966.

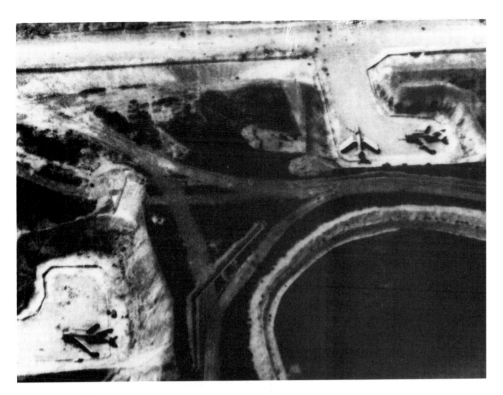

6-43 A reconnaissance photograph shows three Russian-built MiG-17s behind protective revetments at Phuc Yen airfield, 20 miles northwest of Hanoi. U.S. pilots were frustrated that they were not permitted to attack the airfields.

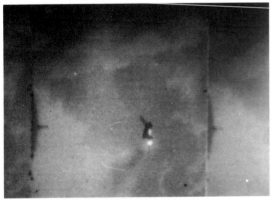

6-44 A North Vietnamese MiG-17 disintegrates under 20mm cannon fire from an F-105D of the 34th Tactical Fighter Squadron on August 13, 1966.

6-45 Gregory "Pappy" Boyington, top-scoring Marine ace of Pacific War fame, poses for a photograph with the men of his old squadron.

6-46 Plumes from the explosions of 750-pound bombs dropped by F-105 Thunderchiefs blossom skyward from he Xuan Mai Army Barracks and Supply Center during an attack on April 19, 1967.

6-47 F-105 Thunderchief pilots deliver their ordnance onto Hanoi's railyard car repair and storage facility, 2-1/4 miles northeast of the city center during May 1967.

6-48 Col. Robin Olds, a fighter pilot whose career extended back to the Second World War II, examines ordnance mounted under the wing of his F-4C prior to a mission over Vietnam in 1967. This aircraft is loaded for an air-to-ground mission. Often, the F-4s would load up with air-to-air missiles to fly MiG cover for the air-to-ground missions.

6-49 Col. Jack M. Broughton, Deputy Commander of the 355th Tactical Fighter Squadron, congratulates F-105 ("Thud") pilot Maj. William J. Bailey, who has just returned from his 100th mission over Vietnam. Bailey donned a portion of his World War II flight gear to mark the occasion.

6-50 Maj. Ralph L. Kuster of the 13th Tactical Fighter Squadron races toward an enemy MiG-17 at 200 knots closure speed during a wild dogfight over North Vietnam on June 3, 1967.

6-51 An F-100 cuts loose a salvo of folding-fin rockets into a Vietcong position in South Vietnam during July 1967.

6-52 North Vietnamese military personnel and civilians savor the moment as they parade a recently shot down American aviator into captivity.

6-53 Manacled together, two American fliers are put on display before angry, jeering North Vietnamese during July 1967, prior to their delivery to authorities for interrogation. Supported by his compatriot, the man at right appears dazed and injured.

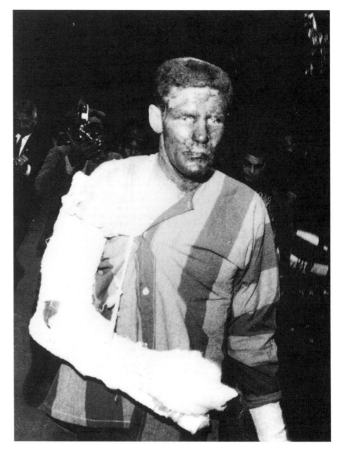

6-54 His broken right arm and multiple burns eliciting no sympathy from the crowds, Lt. David C. Rehman is paraded before a hostile North Vietnamese public.

6-55 American prisoner of war Navy Lt. Paul Galanti provides a very much coached and coerced film interview.

6-56 Empty shell casings from the 8-inch guns of *Newport News* (CA-128) litter the heavy cruiser's forecastle during bombardment in support of I Corps Marines in the DMZ during the latter months of 1967.

6-57 On board the aircraft carrier *Canberra* (CAG-2), sailors in the plotting room work out a firing solution for a target on the Vietnamese shore.

6-58 Smoke and flame belch from the 6-inch guns on *Galveston* (CLG-3) as six more shells hurtle toward a target in Vietnam.

Chapter 7
Life in a Strange Land

Arrival at an overseas debarkation port always had a certain sameness. There were the newcomers (7-1) facing another segment of life with unease, indifference, or anticipation, depending on their personalities and their destinations. There were a few old-timers, returning from leave or for a second hitch, perhaps willing to give a few words of advice to a new arrival. And there were the harassed port personnel, trying to keep everything moving smoothly.

A U.S. Army group moving through Tan Son Nhut Air Base piled into a bus en route to Long Binh Post (7-2) immediately discovered that at least one thing was different in Vietnam. The military had placed screens over the bus window, not to keep the troops from littering, but to prevent guerrillas from tossing hand grenades into the bus.

Arrival at the 90th Replacement Battalion reception station (7-3) initiated the next step in processing. At Long Binh, it was evident that whatever shortage might exist, it was not paper; there were always forms to fill out (7-4). Finally free of the paper jungle, the men moved on to the Central Issue Facility to receive their field equipment (7-5). This was when reality began to set in.

7-1 Welcome to Vietnam. Newly arrived troops disembark from an aircraft at Cam Ranh Bay's 14th Aerial Port.

7-2 Arrivals from Tan Son Nhut Air Base ride by bus to the 90th Replacement Battalion at Long Binh Post.

7-3 Troops arrive from their bus ride at the 90th Replacement Battalion reception station.

7-4 Processing begins at Long Binh with a stack of forms.

7-5 Men of the 1st Cavalry Division (Airmobile) draw field equipment from the Central Issue Facility of the 266th Supply and Service Battalion at Long Binh.

7-6 A Navy Seabee muscles a load of concrete during construction at Chu Lai.

7-7 Cam Ranh Bay's South Beach, seen here in a view looking north in June 1966.

7-8 A panorama of the gasoline tank farm facility at Cam Ranh Bay. When America first joined the war, there were almost no runways in the region that could support American aircraft. A massive building effort was necessary.

The newly arrived soldier could not help but be impressed by the nature and extent of the American commitment to South Vietnam. Ongoing construction and enlargement of facilities was readily apparent (7-6). Typical of the tracts of land that the Americans were transforming and building up was the area north of Cam Ranh Bay's South Beach (7-7). The gasoline tank farm at Cam Ranh Bay (7-8) testified to the enormous need for fuel;Da Nang offered further impressive evidence of the American presence (7-9).

On stateside—and indeed on most overseas—posts, the military police were a relatively unobtrusive feature. In Vietnam, however, they seemed to be everywhere. They even escorted bus travelers to ensure that no one left or boarded the bus as it passed through villages (7-10).

For incoming American soldiers, modes of transportation to their units in the field varied (7-11), but the rides always provided eye-opening experiences. The beauty of the country, contrasting so sharply with the poverty of the people and the primitive roads and infrastructure, reinforced the feeling that this was truly a foreign land where anything could happen.

For many of the soldiers, their new "home" was a fire base (7-12). The men regarded these bases with mixed emotions. On the one hand, they provided some measure of security; on the other, they were remarkably like jails in reverse, where the prisoners were kept inside not to protect the community from the prisoners but to protect the prisoners from the community. The situation can only, at best, have been bewildering to the sol-

7-9 The deep water port and property disposal operation at Da Nang.

7-10 Military Police escort travelers through the village of An Phu.

dier on his first tour of duty in Vietnam. The Americans were neither a conquering army nor an army of occupation, in which case a certain amount of resistance from the natives was to be expected, even admired. But the Americans were supposed to be here as allies.

The ironic prospect of having to be protected against a hostile "friendly" population soon took a psychological toll on the soldiers, who came to regard themselves as vulnerable and isolated. Experience taught them that straying from these bases, or any other installation, could mean certain trouble and often death from booby traps, poisoned food and drink, and a host of other dangers. For example, when their craving for iced drinks led them to purchase ice from the locals, some soldiers suffered severe cuts from ice laced with glass shards.

Soldiers often wrote home about the cratered, desolate appearance of their bases (7-13). For security reasons, all vegetation had been destroyed for a considerable distance out from the installations; sandbags and barbed wire added to the bleak panorama (7-14). Photograph 7-15 pictures the living quarters at Fire Base Jerre in December 1969. Believe it or not, this photograph shows the facility at its best, having been taken during the dry season. At Fire Base Sabre, this view of the briefing room displays the improvised nature of such facilities (7. 16).

7-11 A convoy moves along the road leading to Duc Pho from Chu Lai.

7-12 An aerial view of Fire Support Base Sedgewick of the 25th Infantry Division located near Cu Chi, seen on August 11, 1969.

7-13 Land clearing operations at Fire Base Eunice.

7-14 Sand-bagged buildings at Fire Support Base Black Hawk. Note the barbed wire obstructions in the distance.

7-15 View of Fire Base Jerre showing dugouts and tents used as living quarters in December 1969.

7-16 The open-air briefing "room" at Fire Base Sabre.

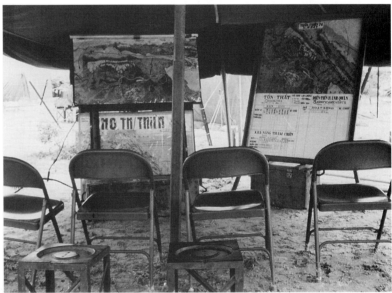

7-17 Thomas Bridges of the 119th Light Infantry Brigade prepares a meal for the men of his unit at Fire Support Base Eagle. Admiring his handiwork are (left to right) SP4 Larry Simple and SP4 Willie Rose.

7-18 Sgt. Ed Densen of the 27th Infantry, 25th Infantry Division, opens a pack of C-ration cocoa at the end of the day's work during a search-and-clear operation near Fire Support Base Kien on August 10, 1970.

As might be expected, the quality of meals for the troops in Vietnam varied, depending on location and conditions (7-17). C rations were served for emergencies or as snacks, according to the circumstances (7-18). On special occasions such as Thanksgiving, the men in the field occasionally received hot meals (7-19).

Many American servicemen were loathe to sample the local culinary products because the food was so different from the cuisine with which they were familiar. Many dishes smelled heavily of fish (7-20), and much Vietnamese food would have seemed spoiled to the Americans, particularly the fruit and vegetables, which often were so ripe that an American chef might have thrown them out (7-21). Many U.S. servicemen in Vietnam during the 1960s and 1970s would not have believed that in the not-too-distant future Vietnamese restaurants would be so popular in America.

Recreation had its place. The armed forces radio provided musical and other entertainment (7-22), but nothing took the place of mail from home, the universal lifeline of a soldier. Possibly no one who has not served overseas in the armed forces, particularly in a combat zone, can understand how much it means to hear one's name sung out at mail call (7-23).

7-19 SSgt. William George hefts a turkey drumstick onto the plate of SP4 Roy Wiley of the 1st Cavalry Division (Airmobile) during a meal on Thanksgiving 1967. Wiley's equipment was typical of the "grunt": "steel pot" helmet with camouflage cover, M-16 rifle, load-bearing equipment, and protective mask.

7-20 An ARVN mess cook prepares a batch of small fish for conversion into nuoc mam sauce, a standard element of the Vietnamese diet.

7-21 Vietnamese support troops of the 50th Political Warfare Battalion enjoy their noonday meal in their battalion's newly constructed dining hall in Saigon.

7-22 GOOD MORNING, VIETNAM!! SSgt. Richard A. Van Dorn, Radio Production Chief of Da Nang Armed Forces Radio, "spins the wax" during a musical program on February 1, 1968.

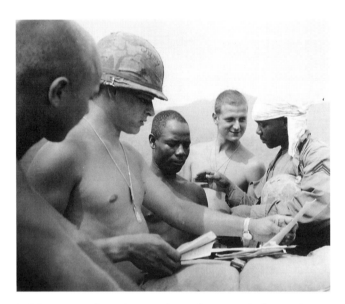

7-23 Letters from home cheer the men during mail call at Landing Zone Stud, a forward base of the 1st Cavalry Division (Airmobile), on March 30, 1968.

The armed forces did their best to provide for the spiritual welfare of the men (7-24). For some, attendance at services was the habit of a lifetime; for others, it may have been their first experience. They went, perhaps with a friend, or perhaps just for something to do (7-25).

Out in the field, the men in the combat units experienced war's harsh reality on a daily basis. In Photograph 7-26, a soldier of the 1st Medical Battalion gives a transfusion to a man wounded in a fight with the Vietcong. A helicopter transported this wounded man to 1st Division Headquarters near Bien Hoa for further treatment. Being wounded "in the middle of nowhere" was a frightening experience, but nothing was quite so reassuring for a man awaiting evacuation as the "wup-wup-wup" of an approaching Medevac helicopter's rotor (7-27).

Hospitals in the field were not huge facilities like those available in the United States, but they looked fine, as did the nurses, both male and female, to those whose lives were saved and whose pain was eased in them (7-28, 7-29, and 7-30).

For the servicemen, the high point of the year—except for the day he shipped out—was Christmas. Even non-Christians looked forward to it. For one thing, there often was a traditional dinner with all the fixings (7-31). For another, various show business personalities performed for the troops (7-32). And course there would be mail from home—lots of it, cards and letters (7-33).

7-24 A chaplain of the 82d Airborne Division tends his flock at Camp Eagle during April 1968.

7-25 Men of the 101st Airborne Division take time out from Operation Van Buren in late January 1966 for religious services in the field.

Christmas always meant Bob Hope, who was in a class by himself. He had entertained the fathers of these men during World War II, their older brothers in Korea, and they knew he would be there (7-34). He and his troop not only played the major bases, but also went "on the road" and played to many a soldier in the field (7-35).

Throughout the year, some of the men might enjoy a break through the R&R (rest and recreation) program. Photograph 7-36 shows soldiers of the 7th Cavalry awaiting transportation to the R&R center at Vung Tau Airfield, which had a beach where the men could relax and swim (7-37).

Despite the best efforts of the military for the safety, welfare, and morale of the troops, service in Vietnam, even aside from combat, was a grim experience. To be risking one's life day after day in a war that seemed to go nowhere, on behalf of a people who seemingly could not care less whether they won or lost, where one hesitated to leave one's base for fear of being killed, when even the folks back home were at best indifferent and at worst hostile to one's mission—this was a sensation bound to lower morale. As always, prostitution flourished wherever servicemen were located.

What was not to be expected was the frightening upsurge in the use of illicit drugs (7-38). A really effective crackdown apparently was not considered political-

7-26 At Ben Cat, about 50 miles north of Saigon, a corpsman of the 1st Medical Battalion administers a transfusion to a wounded man.

7-27 A UH-1D takes off to airlift an injured member of the 101st Airborne Division near the DMZ.

7-28 The 93d Evacuation Hospital at Long Binh in the fall of 1967.

7-29 Interior of the Tuy Hoa evacuation hospital on July 15, 1967.

ly feasible; too many top Saigon officials were involved, including, it was rumored, Premier Ky. So addiction spread through the American ranks. By 1971, the Pentagon estimated that approximately 30 percent of U.S. troops had at least tried heroin or opium.

Hostility became increasingly common between the Americans and the Vietnamese. Often, the Vietnamese viewed the Americans as insensitive toward, and disrespectful of, Vietnamese customs. For instance, citizens of Hué accused U.S. Marines of deliberately running their armored vehicles over Buddhist family shrines set up in the streets (7-39). While these acts may have been accidental, they did nothing to help reconcile a sometimes suspicious Buddhist population to the government of South Vietnam or to their American allies. The Buddhists were not, as some suspected at the time, procommunist, but they despised the corrupt regime in Saigon and disliked the Americans for supporting it (7-40).

Nevertheless, a substantial portion of the population in the South remained loyal to the government and supported the U. S. presence in Vietnam. In the wake of the rioting in Hué, over 100,000 Catholics gathered from throughout South Vietnam and staged a peaceful demonstration in support of the United States (7-41).

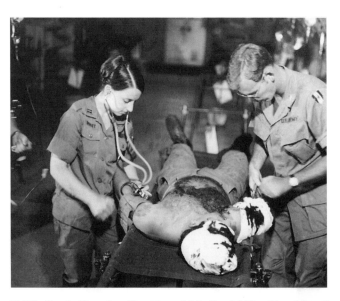

7-30 Capt. Bernice Scott and Lt. David Van Voorhis of the Army Nurse Corps remove field bandages from a seriously wounded soldier sent to the 2d Surgical Hospital for treatment.

7-31 Christmas in Vietnam. Red Cross aides Joyce MacConnackie and Khaki Barden join Lt. Daniel L. Baldwin of the 9th Infantry Division in serving Christmas dinner for troops in the field on December 13, 1967.

7-32 Armed Forces Radio disk jockey Chris Noel performs on camera for the troops during a Christmas Special in 1967.

7-33 Sgt. Craig Anderson of the 7th Marines savors a Christmas card received from home on December 19, 1969.

The gathering, analysis, and dissemination of information was as important in Vietnam as in any other war. The military had its own communications facilities (7-42) as well as intelligence duties, which included translating captured enemy documents (7-43). The ever-hopeful propaganda program kept soldiers busy at such tasks as preparing leaflets to drop over North Vietnam (7-44) and trying to enlist the aid of local villagers (7-45). Neither program was conspicuous for its success.

Press coverage of the Vietnam War was unprecedented in scope. The U.S. military has always respected the right of the press to report to the American people, but always the progress of the war and the safety of the troops had been prime considerations. Thus, a certain amount of control of the press had existed in previous wars, and, to its credit, the press had accepted its share of responsibility. In Vietnam, however, the press, including television news (7-46) was ubiquitous. Valuable space in military compounds was turned over to the hordes of journalists covering the war (7-47). As time went on, the liberal press, always dubious about this conflict, became more and more opposed, and sent home many negative reports.

7-34 Bob Hope, a Christmas institution for three generations of American servicemen overseas, teams up with the Golddiggers at Long Binh during Christmas 1968.

7-35 Members of the 101st Airborne Division enjoy the antics of Hope and company at Camp Eagle on the day before Christmas Eve 1970.

7-36 Seated on their duffle bags, 7th Cavalry soldiers wait at Vung Tau Airfield for transportation to the R&R Center at that facility.

7-37 Soldiers relax on Vung Tau Beach at the R&R Center where there appears to be only one problem—no women!

7-38 A drug raid in Da Nang by Vietnamese civilian authorities nets a room full of drug paraphernalia, opium, and marijuana.

7-39 Buddhist family shrines set up in the streets of Hué.

7-40 Film and office equipment in the rear of the U.S. Information Service Building in Hué, destroyed by Buddhist demonstrators on May 26, 1966.

A development that perhaps no one could have foreseen was the growth of television into something far beyond just another news medium. Never had the truth of the old saying that "a picture is worth a thousand words" been more graphically illustrated. In the newspapers, the public could read accounts of the war's progress or lack of progress, descriptions of the day's actions, and opinions of various officials and commentators. But on television they saw it all with their own eyes—not through someone else's prose. And what they saw were burning and blasted buildings, a devastated landscape, pathetic refugees, and above all, dead and wounded American servicemen. Could any result be worth such a price? More and more, the answer came back: "No!" Gradually but inexorably, the television audience's attitude toward the war became one of horror and disgust, to the point where it could not be ignored. It might not be too much to say that the American news television camera was one of North Vietnam's most effective weapons. As a result, U.S. government officials began to reconsider why we were in Vietnam and how they could more quickly turn over the responsibility for defending South Vietnam to the South Vietnamese.

7-41 A group of marchers hold aloft pro-American signs in English.

7-42 Phu Nom Signal Communications Site located in the Cholon section of Saigon.

7-43 In the Tan Son Nhut area north of Saigon, personnel at the Combined Document Exploitation Center translate copies of captured enemy documents.

7-44 American soldiers packing propaganda leaflets into "bombs," which will be dropped in strategic areas of North Vietnam.

7-45 Using a microphone, a member of the 403d ARVN Political Warfare Company speaks to villagers of Ap Trung, 7 miles northwest of My Tho, about what they can do to keep Highway 4 secure.

7-46 An ABC television news crew unloads their equipment at "The Rock Pile" (Khe Sanh) on October 29, 1967.

7-47 At Khe Sanh, the 101st Airborne Cavalry set up the "Khe Sanh Saloon," a briefing tent and reading room for the news correspondents.

Chapter 8
Reconsideration and Vietnamization

The year 1968 was the climactic year of the Vietnam War. As the year opened, there were a few peaceful scenes to testify to the American military's care for children and the sick. In photograph 8-1, an infantryman is giving an English lesson to some Vietnamese youngsters. A little later, the 199th Light Infantry Brigade held a Tet party for children at a Catholic church school (8-2). And in 8-3 an infantryman carries a sick Vietnamese woman to safety.

At the end of January, however, came the Tet Offensive, so called because its initiation coincided with the Vietnamese New Year celebration. The North Vietnamese called this operation Tong Cong Kich, Tong Khai Nghia (General Offensive, General Uprising—TCK-TKN for short. This ambitious offensive had been in the making in Hanoi for months, in the expectation that it would bring about a decisive victory, thus ending the war.

The offensive was based, however, on the following politico-military premise, which proved to be totally wrong: In the face of a major NVA offensive, the ARVN would turn tail with many desertions; the people of South Vietnam would arise and throw out the Saigon government; and the South Vietnamese would then turn their anger on the Americans. General Giap, who would have to formulate the tactical plans, was very much opposed to the operation on the grounds that it was sure to fail

8-2 Children at the Holy Cross Church School in Bac Hai hamlet clutch candy and C.A.R.E. school packets during a Tet New Year's party hosted by the 199th Light Infantry Brigade on January 28, 1968.

8-1 PFC Stephen Gaye of the 11th Light Infantry Brigade's S-4 Section conducts English classes for Vietnamese children at Duc Pho during mid-January 1968.

and would bring heavy casualties, whereas North Vietnam had been pursuing a successful course. Why change strategies while winning? He could continue to win as long as he did not become involved in a conventional slugfest with an enemy of much greater firepower. But he took up the distasteful duty and produced a grandiose scheme.

Giap's plan visualized attacks on South Vietnamese cities and U.S. military installations, while avoiding U.S. combat troops. The attacks on the cities he assigned to the Vietcong. Unfortunately for the NVA, it lacked the sophisticated communications necessary for the pinpoint coordination of such a massive effort, and a premature attack on six towns, all of which were driven off, tipped off the Americans that the anticipated great offensive was about to begin. The NVA and Vietcong forces lost strategic surprise, but they achieved tactical surprise because they attacked on Tet, a holiday so meaningful to the Vietnamese that very few believed that even communists would violate it. Many ARVN troops were on leave, and those in the target cities were celebrating.

8-3 A member of the 39th Infantry, 9th Infantry Division, carries a sick Vietnamese woman through a muddy rice field to a central medical staging area.

8-4 ARVN troops advance against communist positions in Saigon during the 1968 Tet Offensive while large sections of the city burn, set afire by Vietcong insurgents.

8-5 Nineteen Vietcong infiltrated the U.S. embassy grounds in Saigon after blasting this hole in the wall surrounding the compound.

Saigon was particularly hard hit (8-4). The U.S. embassy was one of the targets. A group of nineteen Vietcong had the assignment, and experienced no difficulty smuggling arms, explosives, and ammunition into the city through the notoriously lax South Vietnamese security. At about 3 A.M. on January 31, the commandos struck, guns blazing (8-5). The four Saigon policemen posted to guard the embassy made themselves scarce at the first sound of firing. Five American soldiers (8-6), and all of the commandos were killed. Over the next couple of weeks, other targets in and around Saigon were attacked, including Tan Son Nhut Air Base (8-7), and an ammunition dump located in a suburb was blown up. Eventually the insurgents were chased out or killed (8-8

8-6 Navy corpsmen wearing flak jackets evacuate an American soldier wounded during the attack on the U.S. embassy on January 31, 1968.

and 8-9). Of course, the Tet Offensive increased the already massive refugee problem (8-10), and attempts to flush out Vietcong guerrillas inevitably resulted in damage to and destruction of property (8-11). Noncombat areas and buildings required as much security as troop locations. At the 3d Field Hospital, SP4 Norm W. Singleton, a patient recovering from a shrapnel wound, volunteered to man the post at the hospital entrance to increase security (8-12).

No city suffered more cruelly during the Tet Offensive than Hué, which the Vietcong and NVA forces captured on January 31. Armed with an "enemies list," they embarked on a savage bloodbath that encompassed anyone with a connection, however remote, to the Saigon government, and many with none at all. The death toll has been estimated at 3,000.

Relief of Hué took twenty-six days of fighting. In this engagement the ARVN fought well, but the U.S. Marines bore the major burden (8-13 and 8-14). Fighting was fierce, much of it at close quarters, and the men grasped at whatever light moment they could experience (8-15). House-to-house combat was the rule (8-16), with the inevitable injuries (8-17). For many of the young Marines, used to fighting in the jungles and rice paddies, this was a new experience. The battle for Hué (8-18) was reminiscent of fighting in the European Theater of World War II in that much of the fighting took place in the city, destroying numerous landmarks (8-19 and 8-20). As the

8-7 The burned-out wreck of a C-47 aircraft lies on the apron at Tan Son Nhut Air Base, a victim of rocket and mortar fire.

8-8 Soldiers move up an M-113 armored personnel carrier and an M-48A3 tank in Saigon during the height of the Tet Offensive.

8-9 A member of the 1st Battalion, 18th Infantry, 1st Infantry Division, pauses at a memorial during a search for Vietcong forces in Saigon's French military cemetery during February 1, 1968.

8-10 February 1, 1968. Members of the 119th Light Infantry Brigade established a refugee camp at Long Binh for Vietnamese driven from their home during the Tet Offensive.

8-11 February 2, 1968. An armored personnel carrier passes buildings that American forces damaged when they rooted the Vietcong from their hiding places in Bien Hoa.

battle for Hué drew to an end, the soldiers' exhaustion became evident (8-21) as well as the heavy damage to the city's infrastructure, caused by the activities of both participants (8-22).

Walter Cronkite of CBS News, already a highly respected and influential commentator, visited Vietnam in February 1968 (8-23). Returning to the States, he proclaimed over national television that Tet was a defeat for the United States. In reality, by the end of the Tet campaign, the communists had suffered enormous losses and had achieved none of their goals. By this time, however, the American press in general was portraying a bleak picture of the military situation in Vietnam. President Johnson had the facts and could have set the record straight about Tet with a few words. But he never spoke those words because by that time he was a frustrated and beaten man. Instead, one month later, he announced that the war would be de-escalated and that he would drop out of the race for president.

Meanwhile, another major battle was under way at Khe Sanh, a U.S. Marine staging area located 14 miles south of the DMZ. Both sides regarded Khe Sanh as an important position. The anticipated NVA attack began early on January 21, resulting in severe matériel losses, including ammunition and fuel; both sides suffered heavy casualties (8-24). The U.S. media compared Khe Sanh to Dien Bien Phu and prophesied defeat, when in fact, unlike the French at Dien Bien Phu, the Marine defenders' firepower greatly exceeded that of the attackers, and the NVA was unable to sever Khe Sanh's supply route. The Marines were well entrenched (8-25), although in some areas a scant 100 yards separated the North Vietnamese trenches from those of the Americans (8-26). By April 1, it was over, the siege lifted, the Marines reinforced. Contrary to many reports, it was not the fiercest, bloodiest battle of the war. Although the U.S. lost 205 killed and 852 wounded, casualties in several other engagements during the Tet Offensive were greater.

8-12 Clad in hospital pajamas and flak jacket, patient SP4 Norm W. Singleton checks a Vietnamese employee's identification card at the entrance to the 3d Field Hospital during 1968. Note that he carries an M-14 rifle.

8-13 Hué during the Tet Offensive. Supported by tanks, Marines move to clear buildings in street fighting near Hué University on February 3, 1968.

8-14 Leathernecks of B Company, 1st Battalion, 1st Marines, aid trapped fellow Marines while under heavy machine-gun fire during fighting in Hué.

The Tet campaign was still in progress when reinforcements began to arrive from the States, including the famed 82d Airborne Division (8-27 and 8-28). Associated units included the 505th Infantry and the 271st Aviation Company (8-29, 8-30 and 8-31).

March 1968 produced a number of notable events. March 1, Clark Clifford (8-32) replaced Robert McNamara as Secretary of Defense. Also, during this month, members of the U.S. 1st Battalion, 20th Infantry, American Division, carried out the massacre at My Lai, to the everlasting shame of the U.S. Army. When it became known in the States, it aroused a firestorm of fury and disgust.

On March 22, Johnson revealed that in June General Creighton W. Abrams (8-33) would replace Westmoreland, who would become Chief of Staff, U.S. Army. The press proclaimed that Westmoreland was being sent to Washington because of the Tet "defeat," but actually the decision had been made a month before the Tet Offensive began.

The trend of thinking in Washington became obvious when the Senior Advisory Group on the war met March 25–26 and advised against additional escalation of the war. And, as mentioned, Johnson announced on March 31 that he would not seek reelection.

8-15 February 4, 1968. Gunnery Sgt. F. A. Thomas of the 5th Marines finds a bit of GI humor in a toy car amidst heavy fighting during the battle for Hué.

8-16 Cpl. Gary D. Keller of the 1st Marine Division fires his M-60 machine gun through a bathroom window on February 6.

For about one week in early May, communist forces renewed their assault on Saigon (8-34). Few histories of the war devote space to this minicampaign, which after the high drama of Tet and Khe Sanh may have seemed insignificant. But fighting was fierce, centering around Tan Son Nhut Air Base, where the Vietcong had set up a position inside the nearby Old French Cemetery (8-35). Action was hot near Plantation Road (8-36). Air strikes and fires devastated much of the area (8-37) and accounted for many casualties. Fires also consumed nearby sectors (8-38) and it became necessary to call in heavy support (8-39). Major structures such as the bridge linking the suburbs of Cholon and Gia Dinh province with Saigon, were favorite targets of communist sappers. The area surrounding this bridge saw particularly heavy fighting (8-40). After about a week, the Americans and South Vietnamese prevailed (8-41).

A never-ending problem was how to prevent the Vietcong from taking advantage of the jungle cover, which was so dense that a man could disappear almost as soon as he entered it. One method was defoliation-spraying the jungles from the air with chemicals that withered the vegetation (8-42 and 8-43). This method devastated the environment (8-44) and in the States became one of the most controversial aspects of the Vietnam War. One of

8-17 5th Marine PFC A. D. Crum of New Brighton, Pennsylvania, receives a field dressing from Navy Corpsman D. R. Howe on February 6.

8-18 A Marine from A Company, 1st Battalion, 1st Marines, moves out under heavy machine-gun fire in Hué during intense street fighting on February 9.

8-19 A portion of Hué's destroyed marketplace, seen on February 14, 1968.

these herbicides was Agent Orange, so called from the identifying orange stripe on its drums. This chemical contained small amounts of dioxin, suspected of causing cancer and genetic disorders. For years the government played down the effects of these chemicals, but Agent Orange was later identified as the cause of these and other ills.

Despite the assurance of de-escalation, fighting went on unabated (8-45) as new troops and matériel arrived (8-46). Events on the home front had been edging toward de-escalation. Peace talks began in Paris on May 12 with Averell Harriman heading the U.S. delegation. These talks went nowhere and would not for more than three years. In August, the Democratic Party chose as its presidential nominee Sen. Hubert H. Humphrey, to the accompaniment of riots in Chicago's streets and the noise of antiwar demonstrators.

To further the negotiations and placate the "dove" faction of his party, Johnson, after due consideration, on October 31 ordered a halt to all bombing raids over North Vietnam. Johnson later came to believe this move had been a mistake because it gave Hanoi a major victory without the U.S. receiving anything in exchange. Under the circumstances, it is ironic that the electorate chose Richard M. Nixon, a confirmed anticommunist, over the liberal Humphrey (8-47).

8-20 Men of the 2d Battalion, 5th Marines, relax in front of a bullet-scarred building and light up cigarettes during a lull in the battle for Hué on February 18, 1968.

8-21 A weary Marine collapses in a heap on the front of his Ontos armored vehicle during a lull in the fighting in Hué on February 23, 1968. The Ontos carried four 106mm recoilless rifles.

Before the bombing halt went into effect, the air war had resulted in increasing losses of men and aircraft, and more American aviators swelled the population of North Vietnamese prisoner-of-war camps. Some pilots, such as Lt. Col. Cecil G. Forster, were more fortunate. He landed his F-4 safely at Da Nang, despite a large hole in one of his aircraft's wings (8-48). Mounting losses kept rescue personnel on continuous standby (8-49), but despite their best efforts, many downed pilots fell into the hands of the North Vietnamese, who delighted in parading captured airmen before the public and displaying them for the international press (8-50).

Although the land and air war received the most publicity, action afloat continued. As the war moved into 1969, air and sea operations focused primarily on Laos and South Vietnam (8-51 and 8-52).

South Vietnam's many rivers were important to its economy and defense. A special organization combining the army and navy, the Mobile Riverine Force, had the task of keeping the rivers out of Vietcong hands. Some of the action was reminiscent of the Mississippi River campaigns of the American Civil War, where monitors patrolled the streams and their shores (8-53 and 8-54). Flagship of the Mobile Riverine Force was *Benewah*, a self-propelled barracks ship (8-55 and 8-56), which also

8-22 Seen on February 28, a bridge lies collapsed in the Perfume River in Hué, blown up by North Vietnamese sappers earlier in the offensive.

8-23 Walter Cronkite of CBS News interviews a Vietnamese professor of the University of Hué on February 20, 1968.

served as a tender and support base for the men and their assault craft. Sea Air Land (SEAL) teams, trained and equipped to conduct paramilitary operations, including surveillance and reconnaissance, also participated in the river warfare (8-57), and a team leader, Lt. (j.g.) Robert Kerrey, received the Medal of Honor (8-58).

Back home, the "doves" who had feared, even expected, that the inauguration of Richard Nixon on January 22 would result in upscaling the war, were disappointed—or gratified, as the case might be—when matters continued much as usual. The soldiers in Vietnam continued to be frustrated by the Vietcong's ability to disappear into the brush and jungle, and sometimes used dogs to track Vietcong soldiers (8-59).

On February 22, exactly one month after Nixon's inauguration, Hanoi embarked on an offensive that apparently had as much a political as military objective. More American casualties would mean more American dissent, and the action would force Nixon into the open, giving

8-24 Marines blast away with a 105mm howitzer at the North Vietnamese forces surrounding Khe Sanh in January 1968.

8-25 An interior view of one of the many defensive fighting trenches held by Marines at Khe Sanh.

8-26 A forward observer at Khe Sanh looks for signs of enemy activity in the distance.

8-27 MSgt. Charles Wunderlich of the 82d Airborne Division's 3d Brigade reads a newspaper on February 14, 1968, during his unit's flight to Vietnam.

8-29 Newly arrived troops of the 505th Infantry, 82d Airborne Division, stand watch during the search of a Vietnamese house near the divisional base camp on February 25, 1968.

8-28 Burdened with dufflebags and equipment, soldiers of the 82d Airborne Division exit the rear of a C-141 transport at Chu Lai Marine Corps Air Station in mid-February 1968.

8-30 Crewmen on board an *Essex*-class aircraft carrier prepare a CH-47B Chinook of the 271st Aviation Company for its flight into Vietnam on February 25, 1968. The helicopter has been pulled off the elevator and forward on the flight deck where the rotors will be installed. Note the covered catapult on the deck at left.

8-31 Maj. John P. Obermire leads the 271st Aviation Company out of their LCS landing craft onto the beach at Vung Tau.

8-32 Clark Clifford, who on March 1, 1968, replaced Robert McNamara as secretary of Defense.

8-33 General Creighton W. Abrams, who replaced General Westmoreland as commander, MACV.

8-34 Saigon firemen pick up the body of a dead Vietcong soldier following an attack on that city during May 6, 1968.

8-35 From atop a tank located on the southwest perimeter of Tan Son Nhut Air Base on May 7, soldiers fire a .50-caliber machine gun into a Vietcong position inside the Old French Cemetery.

Hanoi an idea of what kind of opposition they could expect from the new president.

This offensive was directed primarily against Americans (8-60 and 8-61). This time, however, U.S. intelligence had a good fix on the NVA and Vietcong plans, and U.S. troops had little difficulty thwarting the offensive.

Nixon wasted little time in sending officials to Vietnam to assess the military situation (8-62 and 8-63). He wanted to retaliate against the February attacks, but the alternatives seemed excessive. Then he authorized a B-52 attack on Base Area 353, site of COSVN (Central Office for South Vietnam), North Vietnam's major headquarters for operations against South Vietnam. Because COSVN was located across the border from South Vietnam in Cambodia, when the location of the bombing was publicized dissenters in the United States protested vigorously, even more strongly than Cambodia or North Vietnam.

Several U.S. operations were under way during May (8-64), but it was obvious that, however slowly, the momentum was winding down. In March, Secretary of Defense Laird

8-36 Vietnamese Air Force troops lift a wounded comrade into a trench near the center of the Old French Cemetery during the heavy fighting off Plantation Road on May 7.

8-37 Bodies of three enemy soldiers litter the street just off Plantation Road during the battle that raged in and around the Old French Cemetery.

8-38 Fires set by Vietcong sappers burn out of control on the Newport side of the Tu Duc Bridge in Saigon during May 8, 1968.

8-39 An M-48 tank of the 25th Infantry Division backs into blocking force position on a Saigon street during the North Vietnamese and Vietcong attack on the city on May 8.

announced the program called Vietnamization, whereby the South Vietnamese would be readied to take over their own defense. At best it was an embarrassing situation—the United States would pull out gradually, and had at least to make a pretense that it was not simply abandoning South Vietnam.

On June 8, Nixon announced that he was withdrawing 25,000 troops from Vietnam. In July, elements of the 9th Division began preparing for departure. There were the traditional ceremonies (8-65 and 8-66), as well as preparations for withdrawal (8-67 and 8-68). In late July, Nixon visited the troops in Vietnam (8-69), and by October, many units were in the midst of the much-welcomed redeployment (8-70). Their enjoyment and anticipation were sobered, however, by the recollection of the many comrades who could not join them on the way home (8-71). And many were left behind to go about such dangerous duties as mine clearing (8-72 and 8-73) which could result in some of the most heartbreaking of war casualties—those incurred after the major fighting was over, when total withdrawal was imminent. The question was, how long would it take?

8-40 Spanning the Saigon River, the "Y" Bridge linked the suburbs of Cholon and Gia Dinh province with Saigon.

8-41 Members of the 47th Infantry proudly display a flag captured during a house-to-house search of the areas south of the Kinh Doi Canal and the "Y" Bridge during final mopping-up operations outside Saigon on May 13, 1968.

8-43 After completing their mission, C-123s pull into a maintenance area at Bien Hoa Air Base.

8-42 C-123 aircraft of the 12th Air Commando Squadron flying in formation spray defoliant chemicals on a jungle area east of Saigon on June 7, 1968.

8-44 Jungle areas following defoliation operations.

8-45 PFC Tracy Gray rams an artillery round into the tube of a 105mm howitzer, assisted by gunner PFC John L. K. Alston during 9th Infantry Division operations in the My Cong River complex in June 1968.

8-47 The political changing of the guard. President-elect Richard M. Nixon's incoming secretary of Defense, Melvin R. Laird, confers with his outgoing counterpart, Clark M. Clifford, on December 13, 1968. The portrait in the background is that of former secretary James V. Forrestal.

8-46 Troops of the 131st Engineering Company unload their cargo from a landing craft onto the beach at Vung Tau on September 21, 1968. *Mormacaltair*, a Military Sea Transport Contract Freighter, stands by offshore in the distance.

8-48 Lt. Col. Cecil G. Foster, commander of the 390th Tactical Fighter Squadron, counts his blessings as he stands up through a hole in the wing of his F-4 Phantom damaged by antiaircraft fire during a mission in August 1968.

8-49 Two A-1 Skyraiders of the 6th Special Operations Squadron fly protective cover for an HH-3E helicopter of the 37th Aerospace Rescue and Recovery Squadron.

8-50 Bandaged and disconsolate, U.S. Air Force Lt. Col. J. L. Hughes is escorted through a park in Hanoi in May 1969.

8-51 The nuclear-powered aircraft carrier *Enterprise (CVA (N)-65)* steams in the waters off Indochina.

8-52 Veteran of two previous wars, the battleship *New Jersey (BB-62)* fires its main battery into a North Vietnamese position near the Vietnamese coast during 1969.

8-53 Monitors of the 2d Brigade, Mobile Riverine Force, 9th Infantry Division patrol the Song Ba Lai River on April 14, 1968.

8-54 A Riverine Force crewman trains his M-60 machine gun at a suspicious object on shore while traveling at high speed up the Song My Tho River near Dong Tam on 29 January 1969.

8-55 Aerial view of the barracks ship *Benewah*. Note its brood of monitors and landing craft nested alongside.

8-56 On the fantail of *Benewah (APB-35)* sailors man a 40mm quadruple mount while on patrol in the Giad Due area during April 16, 1968. Note the empty shell casings visible in the gun tub at lower left.

8-57 A SEAL team's outboard-motor assault boat speeds down a branch of the Mekong River with its squad of commandos.

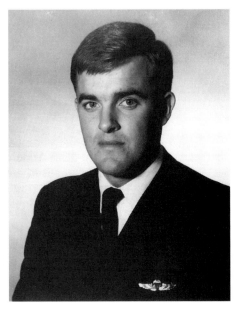

8-58 SEAL Team Leader Lt. (j.g.) Robert Kerrey, later a U.S. senator, was awarded the Medal of Honor for action against Vietcong forces in South Vietnam. Kerrey's team attempted the capture of an enemy political cadre located on an island near Nha Trang.

8-59 A combat team of the 4th Infantry Detachment (War Dog Provisional) sets out on the trail of a fleeing enemy on February 18, 1969.

8-60 In response to a Vietcong attack on Long Binh Post, members of the 1st Squadron, 11th Armored Cavalry Regiment, move out in their M-113 armored personnel carrier to pursue the Vietcong, after taking a short break in a Vietnamese cemetery during February 23, 1969.

8-61 PFC Charles W. Lowery of the 52d Artillery Group arms a 155mm projectile with a fuse at his unit base in Pleiku on March 6, 1969

8-62 Secretary of Defense Melvin Laird greets a squad of Marines of the 1st Marine Division following his arrival in Da Nang during his visit to the I Corps area on March 9, 1969.

8-63 Secretary of State William P. Rogers listens while members of the 3d Reconnaissance Battalion, 3d Marine Division, explain the mission of reconnaissance patrols in the north sector of I Corps.

8-64 Members of the 77th Artillery, 25th Infantry Division, direct their 105mm howitzer fire from Fire Support Base Sedgewick in support of an infantry operation during May 2, 1969.

8-65 South Vietnamese General Cao Van Vien presents the Vietnamese Cross of Gallantry and the Civil Action Honor Medal to Maj. Gen. Harris W. Hollis, former commanding general of the 9th Infantry Division at Dong Tam on July 5, 1969. Elements of the 9th Division took part in a stand-down and redeployment during July.

8-67 Dong Tam during the 9th Division's stand-down. A truck of the division's 2d Brigade carrying communications equipment from the Ben Tre Base Camp enters the town, preparing for the unit's withdrawal.

8-66 An American color guard lowers and folds the flag at Fire Support Base Danger as part of the stand-down of the 4th Battalion, 39th Infantry, 9th Infantry Division.

8-68 July 13, 1969. A CH-47 Chinook helicopter takes off from Dong Tam, bound for Bien Hoa Air Base, while participating in the withdrawal of the 9th Division from Vietnam.

8-69 With high hopes for an American "Generation of Peace," President Nixon greets U.S. ground forces during his trip to the Far East on July 30, 1969.

8-70 By October 1969, many units were in the midst of the much-welcomed redeployment. Troops of the 1st Cavalry Division (Airmobile) board an aircraft at Bien Hoa Air Base.

8-71 Fronted by helmets, rifles, and boots symbolic of fallen comrades, a brigade chaplain of the 82d Airborne leads a ceremony of remembrance at Phu Lai on Veterans Day, November 11, 1969.

8-72 SSgt. James Craig of the 2d Squadron, 11th Cavalry, gingerly inspects a 22-pound Chinese mine during clearing operations near Quan Loi on December 26, 1969.

8-73 The mine-clearing team returns cautiously to Camp Eunice, 83 miles northwest of Saigon.

Chapter 9
Wind Down, Withdrawal, and Cambodia

Before the presidential election of 1968, the peace talks under way in Paris (9-1) had been of little more than symbolic significance. Understandably nervous, the South Vietnamese largely favored Nixon, who was known to be an ardent anticommunist. Indeed, Averell Harriman—and later former President Johnson—charged that Saigon was uncooperative during the final months of the Johnson administration in hopes that a Nixon victory would mean a stiffening of U.S. policy in Vietnam. The North Vietnamese assumed an air of lofty indifference—the American election would only mean trading in one "imperialist" regime for another.

9-1 Averell Harriman, ambassador-at-large and head of the American delegation to preliminary talks on Vietnam, briefs the press in Paris, France, before the 1968 presidential election.

Nixon's first year in office, 1969, left him with a very favorable public rating for his Vietnam policy. He had promised to de-escalate and had done so, bringing home thousands by the end of the year. U.S. military strength had reached its peak of 543,400 on April 30, 1969; by December 31, the figure stood at 475,200.

In early 1970, however, ratings plummeted as the result of an unexpected development. General Lon Nol, prime minister of Cambodia, and the National Assembly ousted the country's ruler, Prince Norodom Sihanouk. The latter had permitted the North Vietnamese to establish bases on Cambodian soil, and to use the port at Sihanoukville, which gave them a means to resupply communist forces in the southern part of South Vietnam. Sihanouk for some time had been establishing closer ties to the Chinese when Lon Nol and his supporters ousted him. They barred the communists from the port and hoped to chase them from their bases. Hanoi reacted promptly and vigorously, sending its forces toward Phnom Penh, the capital.

This development placed the Americans in an uncomfortable position. If the North Vietnamese took Cambodia, they would have not a few bases, but the entire country to use as a sanctuary and springboard into South Vietnam. On the other hand, supporting Lon Nol actively would extend the war. It was not until April 28, 1969, that Nixon decided to act. Operations in Cambodia began the next day, in twelve major parts; U.S. ground forces participated in two of them. Because of the size of the communist buildup, a major battle seemed inevitable, but after a few sharp skirmishes the communists refused battle and fled. The fighting lasted only until May 3; the time until the formal end of the incursion, June 30, was used to clean up the abandoned bases. The American and ARVN forces captured vast amounts of weapons, ammunition, and other supplies.

From the military standpoint, it was a successful campaign, but dissidents in the States were not interested in military successes. They saw only that Nixon had expanded the war into another country (9-2). Especially on college campuses, some protests turned violent (9-3). ROTC buildings were burned; in a number of cases the

9-2 Abbie Hoffman talking to University of Pittsburgh students (1962).

National Guard had to be called out. Four students were killed at Kent State University in Ohio (9-4). Some 100,000 people demonstrated in Washington, D.C., and regular army troops were called in to keep the demonstration from shutting down the government. In this case, there were no injuries. In late June, the Senate repealed the Tonkin Gulf Resolution.

Faced with the necessity to placate the antiwar element, in July 1970 Nixon named Ambassador David Bruce chief of the U.S. negotiating team in Paris (9-5). On October 8, Bruce proposed a "cease-fire in place." This would have been advantageous to Hanoi because the only allied troops in North Vietnam were prisoners of war, while there were active NVA and Vietcong soldiers in the South. But the communists rejected the proposal, seeing no reason to settle for a compromise when all they had to do was sit tight and let U.S. antiwar sentiment hand them full victory. Henry Kissinger, Nixon's national security advisor, and Le Duc Tho, North Vietnam's senior representative, went through the motions (9-6).

Away from the political and diplomatic shadowboxing, the war in Vietnam proceeded on its dismal way. Vietnamization was a major—if illusory—goal, and included training some students in the United States (9-7). Back in Vietnam, the usual unspectacular but deadly engagements continued, with moments of relaxation few and far between (9-8). A spate of operations with names such as Good Luck, Texas Star, and Wayne Thrust (9-9 and 9-10) began and ended. Action continued (9-11) with occasional small triumphs (9-12 and 9-13). In many instances, U.S. and South Vietnamese forces operated together (9-14 and 9-15).

9-3 Student protest at the University of Pittsburgh (1962).

During the spring and summer, U.S. Marines saw considerable action near Da Nang, in the Charlie Ridge area (9-16) and later in the Picken Forest (9-17). Small South Vietnamese units continued to be active, bringing Cambodian refugees into South Vietnam as part of the Civil Operations and Rural Development Program (9-18) and broadcasting to villagers (9-19). For the majority of the American troops, most of the activity was routine—or as routine as a duty can be in a combat area—the inevitable search (9-20) and minefield clearing operations and the resupplying of units in the field (9-21, 9-22 and 9-23).

The year 1970 had been extremely difficult and frustrating for the American officers and fighting men in Vietnam, who had to fight not only the NVA and the Vietcong but also the poor morale and the ever-increasing apathy of many of their own troops (9-24). Experience has shown that the American fighting man stood with the best, provided he knew and appreciated what he was fighting for, had confidence in his superiors, felt pride in himself and his comrades, and believed that his individual efforts made a difference. By 1970, none of these factors seemed to apply in Vietnam.

According to many Stateside newspapers and newsreels, the war was not only purposeless and unpopular but also positively immoral. As for senior officials in Washington, they seemed more concerned with the opinions of Jane Fonda and assorted college students than with supporting their fighting men. The government had obviously given up the idea of real victory, and was nego-

9-4 Service for Kent State students being held in front of the University of Pittsburgh (1962).

9-5 Ambassador David Bruce, chief U.S. negotiator at the Paris Peace Talks, greets South Vietnam's president, Nguyen Van Thieu. U.S. Ambassador to Saigon, Ellsworth Bunker, stands behind.

9-6 Henry Kissinger (left) and Hanoi's senior representative Le Duc Tho (right) engage in animated conversation during a break in the peace talks at a villa in the Paris suburbs on November 23, 1972. The two men had met for the first time on February 20, 1970, at a clandestine meeting in Paris.

9-7 Vietnamese Air Force students work on the rotor of a UH-1D helicopter during a course on helicopter maintenance at Fort Eustis, Virginia in 1970.

9-8 Richard G. Scalf and Thomas R. Parrott, both medics with the 1st Battalion, 22d Infantry, take time for a game of chess at Fire Support Base Louis.

9-9 Men of the 1st Brigade, 14th Infantry, check map coordinates during Operation Wayne Thrust on January 7, 1970.

9-10 James L. Fisher of the 35th Infantry is prepared for action on the perimeter of his company command post in northwest Vietnam during Operation Wayne Thrust.

9-11 The 155mm howitzers of C Battery, 92d Artillery, lay down a barrage at Fire Base Abby on February 7, 1970.

9-12 A communist flag, an AK-47, a poster of Ho Chi Minh, and a French 7.66mm pistol were among the items captured near the Song An Lae River by American forces operating out of Fire Base Louis, 1 mile north of An Khe.

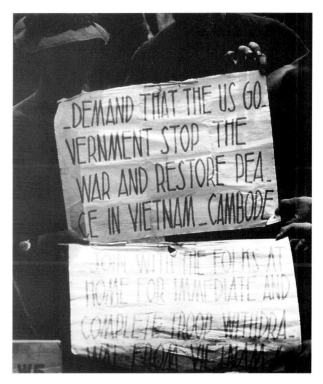

9-13 On their return to Kontum in Vietnam on June 27, 1970, soldiers of the 11th Cavalry hold up a sign found during the incursion into Cambodia.

9-14 Capt. Charles T. Guthrie briefs American soldiers and South Vietnamese Kit Carson Scouts prior to a sweep during a search-and-destroy mission on February 27, 1970.

9-15 During April 1970, Assistant Team Leader Robert C. Todd of Company D, 5th Special Forces Group, mans a .30-caliber machine gun on the bow of an air boat, while a student from the Vietnamese Mobile Force pilots the craft.

9-16 On April 20, 1970, a member of A Company, 1st Battalion, 1st Marines, carries an M-60 machine gun on a search-and-clear operation in the Charlie Ridge area, 15 miles southwest of Da Nang.

9-17 Participating in a multibattalion sweep through the Picken Forest region 25 miles southwest of Da Nang, men of G Battery, 3d Battalion, 11th Marines, stay close to their 105mm howitzer as a CH-53 helicopter lands to resupply their ammunition stores on July 16, 1970.

9-18 Cambodian refugees prepare to disembark from LSU-501 of the South Vietnamese Navy, which brought them from Cambodia on July 23, 1970.

9-19 A Kit Carson Scout of the 8th Psyops Team, 173d Airborne Brigade, broadcasts from Landing Zone English to nearby villages as part of the Chieu Hoi program.

9-20 "Wolfhounds" from the 27th Infantry, 25th Infantry Division, cross a stream 10 miles souteast of Nui Ba Den during search-and-clear operations near Fire Support Base Kien.

9-21 Soldiers follow their equipment and board a C-130 transport at Qui Nhon Airfield on October 30, 1970.

9-22 The "Busiest Man on a C-130." Using a chain lock, Loadmaster T. J. Donegan secures cargo for a shuttle run. When not loading or unloading cargo, loadmasters filled out a myriad of forms for all items and personnel carried on their aircraft.

9-23 A CH-47 Chinook from the 14th Aviation Company lifts off with a sling of fuel drums during a resupply effort to units in the field.

9-24 A soldier with a camouflaged face sits alone with his thoughts during a break in the action late in the war.

tiating with the enemy. Perhaps most maddening of all was the sense of futility. In this weird war, military success was irrelevant. The American forces never lost a major engagement, but they were losing the war.

Under these circumstances, it is not surprising that many a grunt simply gave up. Why risk life and limb in a lost cause? The results were a classic study in what happens when morale and purpose are lost. The number of deserters and those absent without leave (AWOLs) increased as did insubordination and defiance of orders. Some patrols sent out to seek Vietcong sat down as soon as they were out of sight of their post, or "searched" areas known to contain no Vietcong. "Fragging"—the deliberate murder of unpopular officers and NCOs—increased. The men quarreled among themselves. Ethnic, geographical, and cultural differences that with high morale would have been limited to good-natured jibes escalated into bitter and sometimes fatal internecine warfare. Drug use rose sharply, and hard drugs made their appearance. Such disillusioned men lost all sense of personal dignity and went about dirty and unshaven, doing as little as possible. And the situation would be even worse in 1971.

Most of the men kept their equilibrium and carried out their tasks dutifully. Photograph 9-25 shows a helicopter picking up a patrol from the 173d Airborne Brigade, which had just completed a sweep through an area 13 miles south of Landing Zone English on February 16, 1971. Photograph 9-26 shows the beginning of a similar operation in August 1971.

The most significant operation of 1971 was Lam Son 719, designed to cut the Ho Chi Minh Trail and knock out communist bases in southern Laos. This sounded reasonable enough, but there were problems. The Cooper-Church Amendment, which Congress had passed in the wake of the controversial Cambodian incursion, forbade American ground troops and certain support personnel to enter Cambodia or Laos. So the ARVN, with U.S. air support, would have to carry out the ground attacks on the bases. For a few days all went well, although the NVA had learned of the plan, hence tactical surprise was lost. Then the advance came to a screeching halt. Thieu had sent word to Lt. Gen. Hoang Xuan Lam, the field commander, to stop the advance when his casualties had reached 3,000. In constant fear of a coup, Thieu did not want to risk his best units—he might need them

9-25 A UH-1D helicopter from the 61st Assault Helicopter Company lands to pick up members of a patrol from the 173d Airborne Brigade.

9-26 On a search-and-destroy mission during Operation Bushmaster, men of the 501st Infantry, 101st Airborne Division, go out on patrol in support of an attached ARVN Ranger company during August 1971.

9-27 SP4 Roman Capone, 16th Infantry, 1st Infantry Division, cleans his M-60 machine gun as his unit redeploys from Vietnam on February 18, 1970.

in Saigon. This order merely ensured that casualties would be much worse than if the advance had continued, because the NVA brought more and more troops and firepower against a virtually stationary army. From then the situation deteriorated; the NVA bases were not taken and within a week the Ho Chi Minh Trail was back in business.

"Tonight I can report that Vietnamization has succeeded," Nixon stated on national television on April 7, 1971. This was either a deliberate lie or a truly surreal example of wishful thinking. Vietnamization had not succeeded, as Lam Son had demonstrated. The Americans could not kid themselves that they were leaving behind an ally capable of defending itself. This knowledge added to the bitterness of the situation.

Individual soldiers were constantly coming and going (9-27). Troops were not in "for the duration." All enlisted men, including regulars, served one-year hitches in Vietnam, a practice that contributed to the American failure. Instead of a solid cadre of veterans who had come to know and perform their duties almost by instinct, Vietnam saw a steady procession of men who had scarcely grasped the essentials of their jobs before they were whisked home—or killed. Thus, having no personal reason to hasten the end of the conflict, the prime motivation for many a grunts was to stay alive for one year. Most draftees had to serve only one hitch, but the regulars could be and were sent back for second and third tours.

Throughout 1971 and 1972, U.S. forces turned many bases over to the ARVN. Photographs 9-28, 9-29 and 9-30 show some of the ceremonies and mechanics in such a move. Whole units were moving out, equipment was being turned in (9-31), and material was being loaded aboard ship (9-32). Among those headed home were soldiers of the 101st Airborne Division (9-33 and 9-34). Many leaving Vietnam showed up at departure points in fatigues, having come almost straight from the field. Many flights home were on commercial airlines controlled by the U.S. government.

One might reasonably expect that such evidence of disengagement would placate the dissidents. Instead, they grew more vociferous, some of them moving far from lawful and relatively peaceful demonstrations. For example, Rev. Philip Berrigan and several associates were accused of plotting to kidnap Kissinger and blow up parts of government buildings. They were indicted on these charges on April 30, 1971, convicted, and served token sentences.

9-28 Men of the 101st Airborne Division hand over Fire Support Base Tomahawk to the ARVN 5th Regional Forces and render honors to the South Vietnamese flag as it is raised over the base November 15, 1971.

9-29 A captain from the 101st Airborne clutches the American flag after it had been lowered over Fire Support Base Birmingham during stand-down ceremonies in early February 1972.

9-30 Gear and equipment belonging to men of the 101st Airborne awaits transport from Fire Support Base Birmingham after the South Vietnamese took control of the base. Note the crossbow stacked with the M-16 at right.

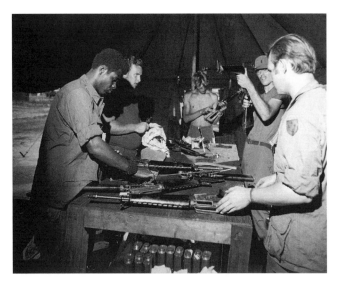

9-31 American Division personnel clean M-16 rifles prior to wrapping and shipping at the Multiple Items Processing Point at Da Nang.

9-32 Tracked vehicles await loading on board the freighter W. B. Waterman at Da Nang's deep water port.

9-33 A happy group of soldiers from the 101st Airborne Division undergo a last search by military police and customs inspectors on January 20, 1972, prior to boarding the aircraft that will fly them out of Vietnam.

9-34 Having cleared the last check point, the men of the 101st Airborne Division quicken their pace into the passenger terminal at Bien Hoa.

In Washington, the Joint Chiefs of Staff met on January 5, 1972 (9-35), with the Marines represented by General Robert E. Cushman, Jr., who had just succeeded General Leonard Chapman as commandant. These men had the unenviable task of overseeing the conduct of a war that all realized was well on the way to defeat.

In an attempt to speed the process and to achieve a military rather than a mere diplomatic victory, on March 30, 1972 the NVA launched the most massive invasion against the South since the 1968 Tet Offensive. Roughly 135,000 men were involved, and this time the Vietcong did not bear the brunt of the fighting; this was almost entirely a professional NVA production, supported by Russian-built tanks and artillery. The scope of this incursion meant that the United States had to take it seriously. In the teeth of the usual pessimism, doubts, and fears,

9-35 The Joint Chiefs of Staff meet in Washington on January 5, 1972. They are (left to right): Admiral Elmo R. Zumwalt, chief of Naval Operations; General William Westmoreland, Army chief of staff; Admiral Thomas H. Moorer, chairman; General John D. Ryan, Air Force chief of staff; General Robert E. Cushman, Jr., Marine Corps commandant.

9-36 The 16-inch guns of the guided missile cruiser *Oklahoma City* pound away at North Vietnamese positions, tanks, and troops along the coast in Quang Tri province during the April 1972 communist offensive.

Nixon acted promptly to increase air and naval forces (9-36). The campaign was long and bitter, and it is generally agreed that U.S. airpower made the final victory possible.

The Da Nang region took a particularly hard beating (9-37 and 9-38). Thousands of people in the Dong Ha and Quang Tri areas were left homeless (9-39 and 9-40), and refugee centers were set up in Hué and elsewhere. In photograph 9-41 we see a B-52 bomber making a forced landing at Da Nang. Saigon itself was again attacked on May 8.

On April 15, American aircraft bombed Hanoi and Haiphong for the first time in four years. As might be expected, the doves raved against this escalation of the air war. It had not been the Nixon administration, but the Hanoi politburo, that had stepped up the pace, but logic seldom has a chance when passions are aroused. Protests were held across the United States, and hundreds were arrested (9-42).

Early in May 1972 Nixon ordered Operation Linebacker I—tactical air support for the ARVN—to isolate North Vietnam from its source of supply, concentrating heavily on port facilities and transportation infrastructure. The North Vietnamese reacted strongly. On May 10, in particular, they challenged U.S. air supremacy, sending up forty-one interceptors. Eleven North Vietnamese aircraft were destroyed; the Americans lost six navy jets (9-43).

9-37 ARVN M-48 tanks take position near the Dong Ha River overlooking Highway QL-9 on April 10, 1972.

9-38 Smoke rises from along the Dong Ha River following air strikes by A-1E Skyraiders on April 11, 1972.

9-39 Vietnamese civilians driven from their homes seek sanctuary in the refugee center located in Quoc Hoc.

9-40 Americans used air power to evacuate civilians from the path of the offensive. Here, evacuees from Kontum run toward a waiting UH-1D helicopter in Kontum's Teneze Compound.

U.S. Air Force crews likewise scored on May 10, 1972 (9-44). Captains Richard S. "Steve" Ritchie and Charles D. DeBellvue went on to become the highest scorers in the U.S. Air Force, both becoming aces. Though they shared four victories together, each man flew and scored with other crews. Ritchie reached ace status first, sharing a MiG-21 with DeBellvue on August 28, 1972. Flying with a different pilot five days later, DeBellvue followed with his second double kill of the war on September 2, becoming the top American MiG killer with a score of six, and the only crew member with multiple kills on separate days.

The Navy aircraft continued to perform well (9-45), but it was the B-52 bombings that were the most effective operations (9-46).

Linebacker II, the so-called Christmas bombings, ran from December 18 to 29, 1972, with U.S. Air Force planes striking Hanoi and Haiphong (9-47). The air force mounted more than 1,000 B-52 sorties, each plane carrying more than fifty bombs. The operation suffered from distorted and erroneous reporting in the United States. Although the primary purpose was political, to make it clear to the North Vietnamese that they had better negotiate in good faith, it also had solid military results. North

Vietnam's military capacity and its industrial base were smashed. Contrary to reporting in the States, civilian casualties were light. And it had the desired diplomatic result—the North Vietnamese returned to the negotiations, whereupon Nixon called off Linebacker II.

On January 27, 1973, in Paris, the U. S., South Vietnamese, Vietcong, and North Vietnamese delegations signed a peace pact; the U.S. Department of Defense announced the end of the draft the same day. In February the exchange of prisoners under Operation Homecoming began (9-48). The Marines had fewer than the other services to await; only 26 Marines had been captured (9-49). There was solemn rejoicing in the home country (9-50). The North Vietnamese, too, had some to welcome home (9-51). Representatives of both governments observed the POW release (9-52). Photographers documented the release of ARVN POWs (9-53). The POW issue is still delicate; many remain convinced that Americans are even now being held in North Vietnamese prisons.

By the end of 1973, all U.S. troops had left South Vietnam, but loose ends remained to be tied up.

9-41 View of a B-52 bomber forced to land at Da Nang in April 1972. Facilities in South Vietnam were not big enough to accommodate B-52 traffic. They operated out of bases such as Guam and used aerial refueling to extend their range.

9-42 Two prominent protestors, Jane Fonda and her husband, Tom Hayden, at a rally held in the fall of 1972.

9-43 Naval aviator and pilot Lt. Randall M. Cunningham and his radar intercept officer, Lt. (j.g.) William P. Driscoll, describe to Secretary of the Navy John Warner and Chief of Naval Operations Elmo Zumwalt the action in which they scored a rare triple MiG kill on May 10, 1972, to become the only U.S. Navy aces of the war.

9-44 Two F-4D crews of the famous 555th ("Triple Nickel") Tactical Fighter Squadron pose for the camera after a dogfight in which they destroyed two MiG-21 fighters. They are (left to right): Weapons System Operator Capt. Stephen L. Eaves and his pilot, 1st Lt. John D. Markle; Weapons System Operator Capt. Charles D. DeBellvue and his pilot, Capt. Richard S. Ritchie. This day marked the first kill of the Ritchie/DeBellvue team, destined to become the only U.S. Air Force aces in Vietnam.

9-45 Post-strike photography of June 26, 1972, documents the results of an air strike by aircraft from *Kitty Hawk (DVA-63)* on the Yen Lap railroad bridge northeast of Haiphong in North Vietnam. Note the cratered bridge approach and dropped bridge span.

9-46 A B-52 bomber takes off from Andersen Air Base in Guam.

9-47 A reconnaissance photograph taken on December 27, 1972, shows petroleum tank cars destroyed by American B-52s in the Kinh No railyard 7 miles north of Hanoi.

9-48 The first group of American POWs to be released during Operation Homecoming muster and report prior to their release to U. S. representatives at Gia Lam International Airport near Hanoi on February 12, 1973.

9-49 Dependents of Marines stationed at Naval Air Station Miramar wait for repatriated prisoners of war to arrive.

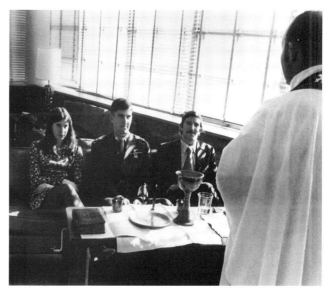

9-50 Family gathers on Sunday during Operation Homecoming on February 18, 1973. The extended family of Capt. James P. Walsh celebrates Mass in the chapel at the U.S. Naval Hospital in St. Albans, New York, while Chaplain James P. McKay presides.

9-51 Operation
Homecoming was
a two-way street. Here,
North Vietnamese
POWs await exchange
and final release at
Bien Hoa Air Base
in late February 1973.

9-52 An army major representing
the United States and members
of the Provisional Revolutionary
Government of North Vietnam arrive
in Bien Hoa for the POW release.

9-53 Members of the U.S.
Photographic Team Pacific
document the release of
ARVN POWs at Loc Ninh.
The photographers (left to
right) are 1st Lt. Joseph T.
Broghamer, SP6 Grant T.
Lingle, SP4 Leroy Massie,
and Sgt. Richard S. Hiwa,
Jr. (the photographer
credited with the previous
two photos).

Chapter 10
The End

10-1 The guided missile destroyer *Henry B. Wilson (DDG-7)*, participant in the evacuation of American personnel from Phnom Penh during Operation Eagle Pull.

On June 13, 1973, a new accord, signed by the United States, North Vietnam, South Vietnam and the National Liberation Front strengthened the treaty of January 27. Two months later, on August 14, the United States officially ceased the bombing of Cambodia, bringing to an end American military action in Indochina.

The real fireworks of 1974, although figurative, were in the United States, where the Watergate drama reached its climax with Nixon's resignation of the presidency on August 9. Gerald R. Ford, the new president, on September 16 proclaimed clemency for the war's draft evaders and military deserters. To the chagrin of many who served, the deserters and draft dodgers got off scot-free. It was the returning grunts who suffered. However gladly their families welcomed them home, an all-too-

large portion of the American people ostracized them as if they were responsible for the war. There would be many bitter days before a more generous attitude prevailed.

On December 13, the North Vietnamese began their final assault on the South. The only wonder is that they held off so long. They also attacked Cambodia, where Lon Nol resigned on April 1, 1975. On April 12, South Vietnam's Nguyen Van Thieu followed his example. One day before, Operation Eagle Pull had begun to evacuate U.S. embassy personnel from Phnom Penh (10-1). The chief medium of evacuation was the carrier *Hancock* (10-2), at the time the oldest aircraft carrier in active service.

There are surprisingly few official photographs of the evacuation operations, and many of those that do (in

10-2 The flight deck covered with CH-53 and CH-46 helicopters, *Hancock (CVA-19)* sails off the coast of Cambodia preparing for the evacuation of American personnel from Phnom Penh on April 10, 1975.

10-3 Phnom Penh, seen on April 12 by Marine photographer D. L. Shearer from the left gunner port of a CH-53 helicopter as it descends toward an impromptu landing zone on a soccer field.

National Archives) are of Marine provenance, credited to one man—Gunnery Sergeant D. L. Shearer. Unless otherwise noted, Shearer took all of the photographs in this series presented herein over a period of nearly a month, from April 9 to May 6, 1975.

These evacuation flights caused considerable anxiety, as Phnom Penh was under siege (10-3), and the helicopters had to refuel and make several trips into danger (10-4). The carrier also took aboard a group of refugee civilians, fugitives from the doomed city (10-5). In the interval between Operation Eagle Pull and Operation Frequent Wind—the evacuation mission from Saigon—the Americans completed the airlift of some 14,000 children. The South Vietnamese government fell, and the North Vietnamese juggernaut moved steadily toward Saigon, preceded by a horde of terrified refugees who remembered the 1968 massacre in Hué.

The attack on Saigon began on April 29, a day when two marines, Cpl. Charles McMahon, Jr., and Lance Cpl.

10-4 Navy personnel wait anxiously on *Hancock's* flight deck for Marine helicopters to complete their return trip from Phnom Penh on April 12.

10-5 Marine Sgt. Chuck McCormick captures a touching moment on film during the evacuation of Phnom Penh, as a fellow Marine holds a refugee baby.

Darwin Judge, were killed by shrapnel from an NVA rocket. They were the last U.S. military personnel to be killed in action in Vietnam. Operation Frequent Wind began the same day to evacuate the remaining American personnel and various South Vietnamese (10-6).

Many South Vietnamese military pilots landed on *Hancock*, seeking refuge for themselves, their families, and their friends (10-7). The evacuees lined up on *Hancock's* flight deck to be searched and processed (10-8) before going below to the hangar deck. Many of those rescued were the humble (10-9), but the formerly powerful were not lacking (10-10). Not all departed on aircraft carriers, as illustrated in photograph 10-11. The airlift from Saigon continued (10-12), but not everyone made it out, because the communist forces concentrated considerable artillery fire on Tan Son Nhut Air Base as they closed in on Saigon (10-13 and 10-14). As the military has done from time immemorial, the Marines improvised, setting down on such impromptu fields as a parking lot (10-15) and a baseball field (10-16).

All day the pathetic stream of evacuees continued under the wary eye of Marines on the lookout for North Vietnamese and rioting locals (10-17 and 10-18). The evacuation came none too soon. At 11:30 on April 30, the red flag of North Vietnam flew over Independence Palace. The long, terrible Vietnam War was over. The U. S. armed forces had known many a tragedy, many a setback, but never before had lost a war.

There was still work to be done. On May 1, helicopters safely retrieved and with a hangar bay full of refugees, *Hancock* headed for Subic Bay Naval Station in

10-6 The first wave of CH-53 helicopters of HMH-463 return to *Hancock* with the first group of evacuees from Saigon during Operation Frequent Wind on April 29, 1975.

10-7 A South Vietnamese pilot lands his Huey helicopter on *Hancock's* flight deck during the evacuation of Saigon on April 29.

10-8 South Vietnamese, American employees, a French nun, and other foreign personnel from Saigon line up on the starboard side of *Hancock's* flight deck.

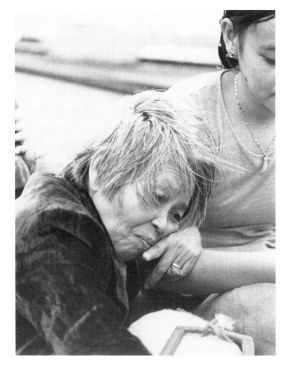

10-9 An elderly Vietnamese woman sits on *Hancock's* flight deck and ponders her future.

10-10 A U.S. Navy photographer catches Air Vice Marshal Nguyen Cao Ky and Lt. Gen. Ngo Quang Truong being accompanied aboard an aircraft carrier following their evacuation from Saigon.

10-11 This navy photograph shows a high proportion of adult males among the refugees crowding the decks and superstructure of the *SS Pioneer Contender.*

10-12 While fires at Tan Son Nhut Air Base burn in the distance, a CH-53 at lower right prepares to set down in a landing zone in Saigon.

10-13 An aircraft burns at Tan Son Nhut Air Base as communist forces close in on the city of Saigon.

10-14 A dozen aircraft lie abandoned at Tan Son Nhut, unable to take off because of the threat of communist SA-7 missiles nearby.

10-15 With the communist forces only miles away, Marine helicopters land in a parking lot in the northern outskirts of Saigon. Note troops deployed among the parked vehicles.

10-16 A Marine CH-53 sets down on a black-topped baseball field used as a landing zone in the northern section of Saigon to pick up waiting refugees on April 29. Troops in the distance provide security.

10-17 Marines of the 1st Battalion, 4th Marine Regiment, keep a watchful eye out while guarding the landing zone.

10-18 Refugees are buffeted by rotor wash as they hurry to board.

10-19 *Hancock* steams for Subic Bay Naval Base on May 1, 1975, with a full load of helicopters.

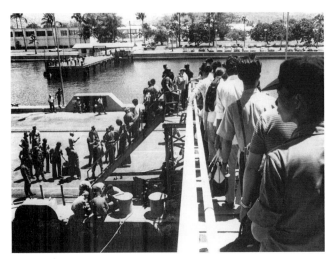

10-20 South Vietnamese refugees from Saigon debark *Hancock* to await transportation to Grande Island U.S. Naval Base, Subic Bay, Philippines, on May 3, 1975.

the Philippines (10-19). Two days later, the refugees debarked to await transportation to Grande Island, with their hopes and fears (10-20). The aircraft carrier *Enterprise*, whose primary purpose was to support the operation, was also at Subic Bay, awaiting the return of its helicopters (10-21) for movement to their home base in Hawaii. Large civilian jetliners also carried many refugees to the United States.

10-21 *Enterprise* lies docked at Subic Bay on May 4, 1975 while awaiting the return of its helicopter contingent.

10-22 Two young Vietnamese girls seem hesitant to leave the bus that has taken them to Camp Pendleton, California.

10-23 Mrs. Virginia Smith (right) and her daughter Sherry (left) talk to Chu Thi Nhan, a friend of Mrs. Smith's son, Norman, who was on his way to the United States from Vietnam.

10-24 Interviewed by the French Press Service on May 6, former South Vietnamese vice president Nguyen Cao Ky sits impassively during a news conference at Camp Pendleton.

On arrival in the United States, many refugees seemed timid, not surprising as they were facing a new life in an alien country, with an alien culture and language (10-22). Some were fortunate enough to have friends meet them (10-23). The press converged on a few prominent individuals (10-24), but most refugees were average families quite content to be inconspicuous. Some had been sponsored by churches, ensuring that they would have security while putting down their first roots in the United States (10-25).

Camp Pendleton in California was a busy place in those days (10-26). There, it did not take long for the refugees to set up their own institutions on American soil (10-27). And typical American hospitality featuring food and music helped make them feel welcome (10-28).

At this time the Vietnamese were a new and strange ingredient for the American melting pot, but in time most major cities would have a "Little Saigon," and such names as Nguyen would cause no more notice than Smith. These new Americans began to make a significant contribution to their communities.

10-25 Do Hai and his wife Pham Thi stand outside their Camp Pendleton quarters with the couple's six children and their sponsors from the First Lutheran Church of Vista, California.

10-26 Marine Private R. D. Shesky of the 1st Marine Division provides a better view of what is going on for a young refugee in Refugee Camp #5 at Camp Pendleton.

10-27 On May 21, 1975, Brig. Gen. Paul G. Graham, Base Commander at Camp Pendleton, shows First Lady Betty Ford a copy of the Vietnamese newspaper being printed by the refugees.

10-28 Entertainment for the newcomers to America. Herb Alpert and the Tijuana Brass heat up a lazy afternoon during a concert at Camp Pendleton on June 10, 1975.

Chapter 11
Aftermath

Even under a communist regime, life goes on at the individual level. No government has ever been able to stop the majestic cycle of life, although some can make that life repressive and miserable. And this the communists proceeded to do for about a decade after the war's end, suppressing private initiative, forcing peasants into collectives, and interning hundreds of thousands of their former opponents in the notorious "reeducation" camps. They also proved that they had nothing to learn from the South Vietnamese officials of the war years about bribery and corruption. Thousands of "boat people" risked their lives and the lives of their families at sea rather than remain in a homeland that had grown unbearable.

Eventually realizing that some changes would have to be made, the communists eased up, permitting a certain amount of free enterprise. Conditions remained very unsatisfactory in the rural areas, but Ho Chi Minh City began to perk up, and it is reported that in general its people are fairly content. The old are grateful for peace, and the young have known no other way of life. Pretty girls flit about, some in Western dress, some in traditional ao dais (11-1).

Photograph 11-1 and those that follow of Ho Chi Minh City and its people were taken early in 1996 by University of Pittsburgh students who formed one of the first groups to go to Vietnam after full diplomatic relations between the United States and Vietnam were established in 1995.

Photograph 11-2 shows a portion of the riverfront, bristling with the advertising signs that are among the least attractive aspects of civilization. These are noteworthy for two reasons. First, they are in the Roman alphabet, not Vietnamese characters. Second, they demonstrate the presence of the Japanese, ever alert to a new market. The Japanese are not the predominant investors in Vietnam, but they are highly visible.

Since the government permitted small private businesses, many set up shop in a very modest way. The man shown in photograph 11-3 is a blade sharpener.

Many visitors from abroad—Thais, Japanese, other Asians, some Europeans and lately Americans—visit Ho Chi Minh City to take advantage of the bargains available in certain goods such as cameras, radios, and clothes. Some believe that the bargains there are better than in Hong Kong. The smiles of the mother and daughter operating their own market indicate that business is booming (11-4).

Typical of the aging population of the city is the old woman in photograph 11-5. She was very friendly to the students who clustered around her as they took her picture. She spoke some English and very good French. She remembered the city in its days of French domination, and recalled the Americans with fondness.

Reminders of the French remain, such as this old headquarters building that the communists have rebuilt

11-1 Young woman of Ho Chi Minh City wearing the traditional ao dai.

11-2 Ho Chi Minh City's riverfront.

11-3 Vietnamese man in business for himself.

and made their own headquarters (11-6).

The riverfront of Ho Chi Minh City could be that of any modern community. There are a few modest skyscrapers, pleasant houses, and good bridges (11-7 and 11-8). Today it is one of the most beautiful cities in Southeast Asia, with one of the best harbors (11-9).

The streets likewise show little of the scars of war. And the many motorcycles are a definite step up from the pedicabs and bicycles of the war years (11-10). Some side streets are devoted to office buildings and small businesses. This one is jammed with motorbikes, mostly Japanese (11-11).

There is only one television station, and it is state owned, so many of the people spend their leisure time reading. Small newspaper and bookstores, such as this one in the old city (11-12) are popular with browsers and buyers. Of course, much of the printed matter is the usual dull communist propaganda, but novels, love stories, and news magazines in French, German, and English are available.

In contrast to the side streets, the main thoroughfares are quite modern and well-kept. By American standards there are few cars to take advantage of the avenues, and most of them, predictably, are of Japanese make (11-13). Probably the Vietnamese would buy American cars if they were available and affordable, as there seems to be little or no prejudice against Americans. Vietnam has

11-4 A mother and daughter smile as they ply their wares in Ho Chi Minh City.

11-5 An old Vietnamese woman recalled bygone days and remembered the Americans with affection.

its own currency, but the dollar is the favored medium of exchange.

The communist regime is relatively tolerant toward religion. It is neither encouraged nor forbidden, and no individual is denied the right to worship in his or her own way. However, blatantly anticommunist religious groups are illegal and their leaders subject to arrest. Fine Buddhist temples, such as shown in photograph 11-14, conduct services as usual. Ho Chi Minh City also has one or two Catholic churches whose parishioners have remained faithful to this religion, which Vietnamese accepted long before the French came. Visitors have noted that most church and temple goers are women and old people, but that situation is not unique to Vietnam.

The United States did not have to rebuild its war damage physically, or endure an alien, repressive government, but the Americans did have to fight their way out of several severe traumas. First and foremost, the United States had gone into Vietnam with the best military in the world, and had come out beaten by a nation with less than one-tenth of America's resources and technology. This was all the more galling because, even hamstrung politically as they were, American troops had won every major engagement. It is small wonder that many grunts came home filled with resentment at the government and people who, as they saw it, had deliberately let them down. They were not entirely incorrect, for some of the doves had been less doves than redbirds, actively encouraging the North Vietnamese to the point that at least touched the border of treason. This legacy of bitterness took years to fade.

The Vietnam War produced a "burnt child dreads the fire" syndrome, with America's leaders and people most unwilling to commit U.S. forces anywhere without a way out. As a result, post-Vietnam commitments were self-limiting, either by a time deadline, a specific mission, or some other well-defined termination point.

Conscription has not been used since the Vietnam War ended. Meant to ensure equitable service in time of war, it did not work that way in Vietnam. There were too many exceptions. For instance, anyone with enough money to hole up in college or run off to Canada was safe. As a result, the burden of the war fell on those less blessed with worldly goods. African Americans, in particular, believed—with some justice—that they may have carried a disproportionate load.

A conviction that some U.S. prisoners remain incarcerated in North Vietnam has led to every major military event in the United States featuring a "missing in action" lamp. It seems unlikely that the pragmatic communists would feed a useless prisoner for twenty-five years when they could rid themselves of the burden by turning him over to the nearest American or European agency—and gain credit by so doing. Certainly there are no more prisoners in the infamous Hanoi Hilton; it has been torn down and replaced with office buildings.

Some Americans have returned from a visit to Vietnam believing that this could be a tremendous new market for the United States. The Taiwanese, South Koreans, and Japanese are already on the scene and doing well. Perhaps it is time to clean the slate and engage in mutually profitable trade with Vietnam.

It has taken the Americans almost as long to forgive each other as it has to recognize Vietnam. The Vietnam

11-6 Rebuilt French headquarters now houses the communist headquarters in Ho Chi Minh City.

11-7 A view of Ho Chi Minh City's riverfront.

11-8 Another section of Ho Chi Minh City's waterfront.

11-9 Ho Chi Minh City's busy harbor.

11-10 A street scene in Ho Chi Minh City.

11-11 Another side street in Ho Chi Minh City. American veterans would find these motorcycles much improved over the thousands they saw in Saigon during the Vietnam War.

11-12 A well-patronized book and newspaper store on a side street in Ho Chi Minh City.

War Memorial stands as a symbol of that healing. Now an acknowledged masterpiece, when the design was first made public, many embittered veterans objected—they had been pushed out of public recognition all these years, and now that they were finally to have a memorial, it was going to be merely a wall with thousands of names inscribed, which should change as more missing in action were confirmed dead.

Such sentiments could not survive a visit to the memorial. The setting is beautiful, the location near other shrines in Washington, D.C. (11-15). Its decoration is simple: name after name of those who fell in Vietnam about 58,000 in all. (11-16). Near the Wall, a statue was erected showing three combat soldiers (11-17). Some objected to this, believing it detracted from the austere beauty of The Wall. Others, however, thought that it humanized the memorial. Today it is accepted as an integral part of the complex. Always at the foot of "The Wall" are touching little tributes—a cap, a letter, some small trinket—meaningful to the one who left them there. The place is never deserted in daylight hours and is probably one of the most photographed sites in Washington. Thousands of Vietnam veterans and their families flock there, to stand in silent contemplation of this evidence that, at last, they are appreciated and honored.

11-13 A main street in Ho Chi Minh City.

11-14 A Buddhist temple in Ho Chi Minh City.

11-15 The entrance to the Vietnam Veterans Memorial, seen from the pathway leading from the Reflecting Pool in front of the Lincoln Memorial.

11-16 A piece of the monument to the American soldiers who served in Vietnam. "The Wall" contains the names of the American war dead.

11-17 With millions of Vietnam veterans still alive, the Vietnam Memorial may well be one of the most photographed structures in Washington.

Selected Bibliography

Bonds, Ray, ed. *The Vietnam War: The Illustrated History of the Conflict in Southeast Asia*. New York: Crown, 1979.

Bowman, John S., ed. *The Vietnam War: An Almanac*, New York: World Almanac Publications, 1985.

Buttinger, Joseph. *Vietnam: A Dragon Embattled*. New York: Praeger, 1967.

———. *Vietnam: The Unforgettable Tragedy*. New York: Horizon, 1977.

Charlton, Michael, and Anthony Moncrief. *Many Reasons Why: The American Involvement in Vietnam*. New York: Hill & Wang, 1978.

Davidson, Phillip B. *Vietnam at War*, Novato, CA: Presidio Press, 1988.

Davidson, William B. *Vietnam at War: The History 1946–1975*. Novato, CA: Presidio Press, 1988.

Duiker, William J. *The Communist Road to Power in Vietnam*. Boulder, CO: Westview Press, 1981.

Fall, Bernard B. *Street Without Joy: Indochina at War, 1946–54*. Harrisburg, PA: Stackpole Company, 1961.

———. *The Two Vietnams: A Political and Military Analysis*. New York: Praeger, 1961.

Fitzgerald, Frances. *Fire in the Lake: The Vietnamese and the Americans in Vietnam*. Boston: Little, Brown, 1972.

Halberstam, David. *The Best and the Brightest*. Greenwich, CT: Fawcett, 1969.

Herrington, Stuart A. *Peace with Honor?* Novato, CA: Presidio Press, 1983.

Johnson, Lyndon Baines. *The Vantage Point: Perspective of the Presidency, 1963–1969*. New York: Rinehart & Winston, 1971.

Karnow, Stanley. *Vietnam: A History*. New York: Penguin Books, 1984.

Kissinger, Henry B. *The White House Years*. Boston: Little, Brown, 1979.

———. *Years of Upheaval*. Boston: Little, Brown, 1982.

McNamara, Robert S. *In Retrospect: The Tragedy and Lessons of Vietnam*. New York: Times Books, 1995.

Nixon, Richard M. *No More Vietnams*. New York: Arbor House, 1985.

———. *The Memoirs of Richard Nixon*. New York: Grosset & Dunlop, 1978.

———. *The Real War*. New York: Warner Books, 1980.

Oberdorfer, Don. *Tet!* New York: Doubleday, 1971.

Santoli, Al. *To Bear Any Burden*, New York: E. P. Dutton, 1985.

Summers, Harry G. *Vietnam War Almanac* New York: Facts on File Publications, 1985.

Vo Nguyen Giap. *People's War, People's Army: The Viet Cong Insurrection Manual for Undeveloped Countries*. New York: Fredrich A Praeger, 1962.

Westmoreland, William C. *Report on the War in Vietnam*. Washington, DC: Government Printing Office, 1969.

Index

UNITED STATES AND SOUTH VIETNAMESE FORCES AND EQUIPMENT

Sources

Bowman, John S., ed., *The Vietnam War: An Almanac,* New York: World Almanac Publications, 1985.

Davidson, Phillip B., *Vietnam at War, Novato,* California: Presidio Press, 1988.

Karnow, Stanley, *Vietnam: A History,* New York: Penguin Books, 1991.

Santoli, Al, *To Bear Any Burden,* New York: E. P. Dutton, Inc., 1985.

Summers, Harry G., *Vietnam War Almanac,* New York: Facts on File Publications, 1985.

Other Brassey's Photo Histories
by Goldstein, Dillon, and Wenger

D-Day Normandy: The Story and Photographs

Nuts! The Battle of the Bulge

Rain of Ruin: A Photographic History of Hiroshima and Nagasaki

The Spanish-American War: The Story and Photographs
(with Robert J. Cressman)

The Way It Was: Pearl Harbor—The Original Photographs

To order these books or to receive a catalog of the many fine titles available from Brassey's, please contact:

Brassey's, P.O. Box 960,
Herndon, Va. 20172
Telephone (800) 775-2518
Fax (703) 661-1501